CONTENTS

Welcome to the Journey — 1
Part 1: Understanding Your True Self — 8
Day 1: Meeting the Real You — 10
Day 2: Identifying the Roles and Masks You Wear — 15
Day 3: Rewriting Your Personal Story — 22
Day 4: The Power of Self-Awareness — 30
Day 5: Discovering Your Core Values — 38
Day 6: Embracing Vulnerability — 46
Day 7: Expanding Your Emotional Vocabulary — 55
Part 2: Strengthening Your Emotional Core — 64
Day 8: The Power of Self-Compassion — 65
Day 9: Setting Healthy Boundaries — 73
Day 10: Releasing Emotional Baggage — 82
Day 11: The Discipline of Self-Care — 90
Day 12: Building Self-Trust — 96
Day 13: Managing Emotional Triggers — 103
Day 14: The Gratitude Mindset — 111
Part 3: Becoming Your Most Authentic Self — 118
Day 15: Reconnecting with Your Inner Child — 119
Day 16: Living with Purpose — 126
Day 17: Expressing Your True Self — 133

Day 18: Embracing Imperfections	142
Day 19: Aligning with Integrity	150
Day 20: Finding Peace in Stillness	159
Day 21: Celebrating Your Journey	167
Conclusion: Your Next Steps	176
Bonus Section: Quick Tools for Daily Self-Connection	184

WELCOME TO THE JOURNEY

First and foremost, I want to acknowledge the significance of this moment: *You've taken the first step toward something deeply meaningful.*

In a world that pulls us in so many directions, filled with obligations, expectations, and distractions, you've chosen to carve out time for yourself.

You've chosen to turn inward, to explore who you really are beyond the roles you play, the goals you pursue, and the pressures you face every day.

That's no small decision—and it's one that could very well change the course of your life. So, welcome. You're exactly where you need to be.

This book isn't just another self-help guide or another item on your growing to-do list. Think of it as a companion—someone who walks beside you on your journey, offering insight, support, and encouragement along the way.

I'm not here to tell you who to be or how to live your life. You already hold all the wisdom you need within yourself. What this book offers is the structure, the tools, and the space to help you access that wisdom, to help you rediscover the person you truly are beneath the layers of life's demands.

If you've ever felt disconnected from yourself—wondering who you are beyond your job, your responsibilities, your relationships—you're not alone. It's easy to lose sight of who we are in a world that constantly tells us who we should be.

Maybe you've been caught in a cycle of self-criticism, feeling like you're not enough, or perhaps you've been so focused on caring for others that you've neglected to care for yourself. These feelings are all too common, but they don't have to define your experience.

The journey you're about to embark on is one of self-discovery, self-compassion, and ultimately, self-connection.

And here's the beautiful thing: you don't have to overhaul your life to find that connection. You don't have to spend hours in deep meditation or change your career or isolate yourself from the world.

The journey to self-connection can happen in small, meaningful moments—moments of reflection, of listening to yourself, of being honest with yourself. It's a journey that fits into your life, rather than asking you to pause everything just to get started.

By the time you finish this book, you'll have a deeper, more grounded understanding of who you are at your core. You'll have developed practices that help you reconnect with yourself even when life gets hectic, and you'll have cultivated the emotional resilience and strength needed to face challenges with grace and self-compassion.

So, let's begin. Together, we'll take this journey one step at a time, and I promise you this: you'll come out of it with a stronger, more authentic connection to the person you've always been.

What You'll Learn

Over the course of these 21 days, we're going to dive into the key pillars that build a strong foundation for self-connection. Each day brings a new insight, a new tool, or a new practice that will help you reconnect with yourself in a meaningful way.

The goal is to guide you through a process of transformation—not an overnight change, but a gradual, intentional shift that will leave you feeling more aligned, more grounded, and more connected to your true self.

Here's a quick overview of the main themes we'll explore:

- **Self-Connection**: At the heart of this book is the concept of self-connection. What does it mean to be truly connected to yourself? It's about knowing who you are at your core—your values, your strengths, your desires—and living in alignment with that understanding. It's about quieting the external noise and listening to your inner voice, allowing it to guide your actions and decisions.
- **Emotional Resilience**: Life is full of challenges, and emotional resilience is what helps you navigate those challenges without losing your sense of self. Throughout this journey, you'll learn how to strengthen your emotional core so that you can face difficulties with grace, rather than feeling overwhelmed or disconnected.
- **Self-Compassion**: One of the most powerful tools you'll develop over these 21 days is self-compassion. Too often, we're our own harshest critics. We beat ourselves up for not being "enough," for making mistakes, or for not having it all figured out. But self-compassion teaches us to treat ourselves with kindness, to forgive our missteps, and to offer ourselves the same love and care we extend to others.
- **Growth and Purpose**: This journey isn't just about self-reflection; it's about growth. As you strengthen your connection to yourself, you'll begin to notice shifts in how you approach your life—how you make decisions, how you set boundaries, how you prioritize your time. You'll also explore what it means to live with purpose, aligning your daily actions with your core values and deepest desires.

By the end of the 21 days, you'll have built a toolkit of practices that you can continue to use long after you've finished this book.

You'll have a deeper sense of who you are, and you'll be better equipped to handle life's ups and downs with emotional strength and resilience. Most importantly, you'll have developed a lasting connection with yourself that will serve as the foundation for everything you do.

Why Self-Connection Matters

It's easy to move through life without ever stopping to ask, "Who am I, really?" We get so caught up in the hustle and bustle —work, family, social obligations—that we forget to check in with ourselves.

We live on autopilot, fulfilling roles and meeting expectations, but rarely do we pause to consider what *we* truly want, what *we* need to feel fulfilled, and whether the lives we're living align with our true selves.

Self-connection is the antidote to this disconnection. It's about coming home to yourself, about remembering who you are at your core and living from that place of authenticity.

When you're connected to yourself, you're able to make decisions that align with your values, rather than being swayed by external pressures or expectations. You're able to set boundaries that protect your energy and well-being, rather than saying "yes" to everything out of obligation.

And perhaps most importantly, you're able to cultivate a sense of peace and fulfillment that comes from within, rather than constantly seeking it outside yourself.

This journey to self-connection is especially important in today's world, where we're often overwhelmed by the sheer volume of information, expectations, and demands on our time. We're bombarded with messages about who we should be, what we should achieve, and how we should look.

It's easy to feel lost in the noise, to feel like we're never doing enough or being enough. But when you're truly connected to yourself, you realize that you *are* enough, just as you are.

You begin to understand that your worth doesn't come from what you accomplish or how others perceive you—it comes from within.

That's why self-connection is so powerful. It's the foundation for everything else in your life.

When you're connected to yourself, you're more resilient, more confident, and more capable of handling whatever life throws your way.

You're able to show up fully, both for yourself and for the people you care about, because you're grounded in who you are.

And that's a gift not only to yourself but to everyone around you.

How to Use This Book

I know life is busy. Between work, family, and personal commitments, it can feel like there's never enough time in the day.

That's why this book is designed to be accessible and flexible, fitting into your life rather than adding more pressure to it.

The structure is simple, and each chapter is designed to be short and to the point—something you can easily read during a break or before bed.

Here's how it works:

- **Daily Lessons**: Each day, you'll explore a new concept or practice related to self-connection, emotional resilience, or self-compassion. These lessons are meant to be practical and applicable, so you can start using them right away in your everyday life.

- **Reflection Prompts**: After each lesson, you'll find a reflection prompt to help you dive deeper into the topic. These prompts are designed to encourage self-inquiry and self-awareness, helping you uncover insights about your inner world.
- **Practical Exercises**: Each chapter also includes a simple exercise that you can practice throughout the day. These exercises are not time-consuming or complicated—they're meant to fit into your routine and reinforce the day's lesson in a tangible way.
- **Tracking Your Progress**: At the end of each week, you'll have an opportunity to reflect on your progress. Personal growth is a journey, and it's important to recognize and celebrate the small steps you're taking along the way. This will help you stay motivated and focused as you move forward.

You don't need to set aside hours of your day to complete this journey. Even 10-15 minutes of reading and reflection each day can lead to significant shifts in how you connect with yourself.

The key is consistency—showing up for yourself each day, even if it's just for a few minutes. Over time, these small, consistent actions will add up to meaningful change.

Starting Point: Your Self-Assessment

Before we begin, it's important to take stock of where you are right now. This self-assessment will help you gauge your current level of self-connection and emotional strength, providing a baseline from which you can track your growth over the next 21 days.

This isn't about passing or failing, and there are no right or wrong answers. It's simply a tool for reflection—a way for you to check in with yourself and notice how you're feeling at the start of this journey.

You might discover that there are areas where you feel strong and connected, and others where you feel disconnected or uncertain. That's perfectly okay.

The purpose of this assessment is to give you a starting point, so you can look back at the end of this book and see just how far you've come.

As you answer the questions, try to be as honest and compassionate with yourself as possible. Remember, this is your journey, and wherever you are right now is exactly where you're meant to be.

Take a few moments to reflect, and when you're ready, we'll begin this 21-day journey of self-connection, resilience, and inner strength.

I'm honored to walk this path with you. Let's get started. *Nice to meet you!*

PART 1: UNDERSTANDING YOUR TRUE SELF

Week 1: Building Awareness and Self-Discovery

This first week sets the foundation for the entire journey. It's about one of the most profound yet often neglected aspects of life—*understanding who you truly are.*

Think of this as the start of a deep, heartfelt conversation between you and your authentic self. Over the next seven days, you'll begin to uncover the layers of conditioning, expectations, and roles that may have kept you from seeing or connecting with your true self.

You'll begin to differentiate between the person you show the world and the person who exists beneath all those layers—the one who is deeply, authentically you.

In the rush of daily life, it's easy to lose touch with that part of ourselves. Maybe you've felt this yourself: the feeling that you're simply going through the motions, fulfilling obligations, meeting expectations, and playing various roles that, while necessary, don't always reflect who you really are inside.

Many people live years, even decades, without ever taking a moment to pause and ask themselves, *"Am I truly living in alignment with who I am?"*

This week is an invitation to begin that reflection. You're here because something inside you knows there's more. More to you, more to life, more to your journey. And I'm here to assure you that there *is* more—so much more.

But first, we need to create the space for that discovery. We need to make room for your true self to emerge, free of the roles and expectations you've carried for so long.

As we go through these first few days, approach everything with curiosity and kindness. There's no rush, no right or wrong way to uncover who you are. It's not about instant transformation; it's about gentle awareness.

And as you begin to reconnect with yourself, you'll start to feel a sense of lightness, as if a weight you didn't even realize you were carrying begins to lift. You'll feel the relief of stepping into your own shoes—those that fit you perfectly.

Are you ready? Let's begin.

DAY 1: MEETING THE REAL YOU

Understanding the Distinction Between Your True Self and the Persona You Present to the World

Today is where we start—where you begin to meet the real you.

This isn't about discovering someone brand new, but rather about reconnecting with the person you've always been, deep inside. Often, without realizing it, we can become distanced from that person, veiled behind the roles we play in our professional and personal lives.

Think for a moment about the masks you wear every day. They're not bad or wrong—masks help us navigate the world.

At work, you might wear the mask of a leader, a professional who's always on top of things. With friends, maybe you're the one who's always listening, always offering support. At home, perhaps you play the role of the nurturer, the caretaker, or the dependable one.

These roles are a natural part of life, and in many ways, they're necessary. But over time, if we spend too much time in these roles, it's easy to lose sight of who we are *without* the masks.

Your true self, on the other hand, is something far deeper. It's the part of you that remains constant, even when you're alone with your thoughts. It's the version of you that knows what makes your heart sing and what drains your energy. It's the part of you that longs to be understood, to be seen, and to live authentically.

And, often, it's the part of you that gets drowned out in the busyness of life, in the noise of responsibilities and external expectations.

Have you ever noticed how, in moments of quiet, you might feel a sense of longing or restlessness that you can't quite explain? Or perhaps you find yourself asking, *"Is this really all there is?"*

These moments are your true self trying to speak, trying to break through the surface and be heard. Today, we're going to give that part of you the space and the voice it needs.

We're going to allow your true self to introduce itself fully—no more hiding behind roles or expectations.

Exercise: Write a Letter from Your True Self to Your Current Self

This exercise is one of gentle introspection. It's an invitation to start a conversation with the part of you that knows you best—your true self.

This is the part of you that sees through the layers of roles, responsibilities, and habits.

It's the part of you that holds all the wisdom, strength, and compassion you need, even when you don't feel it in your day-to-day life.

Here's what you'll do: Imagine that your true self could sit down and write you a letter. In this letter, it would speak directly to the version of you that exists right now—the one who may be struggling with self-doubt, navigating the demands of a busy life, or feeling disconnected from a sense of purpose. What would your true self say to you?

Start by creating a quiet space where you won't be interrupted. This is your time to connect inward, so choose a setting that feels calm and supportive.

Grab a pen and paper or open a journal, and write from the perspective of your true self to your current self. Let the words flow without overthinking them.

To guide you, here are some prompts:

- What are the qualities your true self admires about you?
- What strengths have you shown, even when you felt like you were struggling?
- What advice would your true self give you about living more authentically?
- What is your true self asking you to release or let go of?
- What does your true self long for you to embrace more fully in your life?

This letter is your opportunity to be radically honest with yourself—without judgment, without pressure. It's a safe space to explore the parts of yourself that might have been pushed aside or silenced.

As you write, try not to censor yourself. Let the words flow, and allow your true self to speak freely.

Reflection on the Letter

Once you've finished writing your letter, take a few moments to reflect on it.

How did it feel to let your true self speak? Did anything surprise you? Were there certain qualities or desires that came up that you hadn't acknowledged in a long time?

This exercise is often one of both relief and revelation.

You might feel a sense of lightness from allowing your authentic self to finally have a voice. You might also feel some resistance, especially if your true self is asking you to look at parts of your life that you've been avoiding. Both experiences are valid.

The important thing is that you're beginning to open up the dialogue between your current self and your true self.

This letter is something you can return to throughout the 21-day journey.

As you move through the process of self-connection, you'll find that your understanding of who you are will deepen, and new layers of your true self will continue to emerge.

For now, simply honor what came up during this exercise. Be proud of the fact that you've taken the first step toward reconnecting with yourself.

If you feel comfortable, keep this letter somewhere safe. You may want to read it again in a few days or weeks to see how your relationship with your true self evolves.

Takeaway

Today is the beginning of something beautiful—a reunion with the real you. It's important to acknowledge that this process doesn't happen overnight.

Reconnecting with your authentic self is a journey, and like any meaningful journey, it requires time, patience, and practice.

But by taking the first step today, you've already started to clear the path toward greater self-awareness, emotional resilience, and self-compassion.

Over the next few days, we'll continue to explore the various roles and masks you wear in your everyday life and how these impact your connection to your true self.

As we move forward, I encourage you to hold onto the insights from today's exercise.

Remember that your true self is always there, always ready to guide you back to what matters most.

You are not here to be perfect. You are here to be *you*—and that is more than enough.

Tomorrow, we'll dive into the roles and personas you present to the world and how they shape your sense of self.

For now, take a deep breath, give yourself a moment of gratitude for showing up today, and know that you're already on the path to discovering the real, authentic you.

Welcome to the beginning of your journey. It's truly *nice to meet you*.

DAY 2: IDENTIFYING THE ROLES AND MASKS YOU WEAR

Welcome to Day 2. Yesterday, you began a profound journey—one that asked you to meet your true self, to strip away the layers of external expectations and see the person who exists at your core. It was the beginning of reconnecting with the authentic you, and I hope you felt a sense of curiosity and relief as you started to uncover that person.

Today, we're going to build on that work by exploring the many roles you play in your daily life.

As we move through the world—at work, at home, with friends, and in society—we adopt different roles, often without realizing it.

These roles are like the clothes we wear: they help us fit in, function, and protect ourselves in various situations.

But just like a pair of shoes that doesn't fit quite right, some roles can start to feel uncomfortable over time. Wearing them too long can separate us from ourselves.

*The Roles We Play and
the Masks We Wear*

Think about the various roles you play in your life.

You might be the responsible one at work, the caretaker at home, the problem solver for your friends. Perhaps you're the one who always keeps the peace, even when your inner world feels like chaos. Maybe you're the achiever, the one who's always pushing for more, striving to be the best, yet silently wondering if it's ever enough.

Each of these roles comes with its own set of expectations, some of which you've chosen and some that have been imposed on you by society, family, or circumstances.

While these roles can be helpful in certain situations, they also come with their own set of challenges.

Over time, they can become masks that hide your true self. You might feel pressure to live up to the expectations that come with these roles, and in doing so, you may suppress your true desires, thoughts, and emotions.

The more you lean into these roles, the more you risk disconnecting from the person you really are. It can be exhausting to always feel like you have to "perform," even if it's subconscious.

Take a moment to reflect: Have you ever caught yourself acting a certain way because it's what's expected of you, even though it didn't feel natural or true to who you are? Maybe it was laughing along with a joke that didn't resonate, saying "yes" to something when you really wanted to say "no," or holding back your opinions to avoid conflict.

These moments, while small, add up over time. They become habits, and before long, you might find that the person you present to the world is different from the person you are inside.

It's important to understand that this is not about blame or shame. The roles we play often serve a purpose—they help us navigate difficult situations, meet our responsibilities, and protect ourselves from vulnerability.

But if we never take the time to step back and examine these roles, we risk losing touch with our true selves. We risk living a life that feels more like a performance than a genuine expression of who we are.

Why We Wear Masks

Let's take a moment to explore why we wear these masks.

More often than not, it's because we feel that our true selves might not be accepted, understood, or appreciated by others. We fear judgment, rejection, or failure. So, instead, we adapt. We mold ourselves to fit the expectations of others, whether it's at work, in relationships, or in society.

For example, in a professional setting, you might feel the need to wear the mask of "the competent one," always in control, never showing weakness or doubt. You might be afraid that if you let your guard down, others will see you as less capable. In friendships, perhaps you wear the mask of "the easygoing one," never rocking the boat, always putting others' needs first. You might worry that if you assert your own needs, you'll be seen as selfish or difficult.

But here's the thing: While these masks may protect us in the short term, they also keep us from truly connecting with ourselves and others. When we constantly hide behind a mask, we deprive ourselves of the opportunity to be seen and loved for who we really are. We also deprive others of the chance to truly know us—the real us. And that's one of the deepest desires we all share: to be seen, to be known, and to be loved for who we really are.

Today's exercise is an opportunity to take a closer look at the roles you're playing and the masks you're wearing.

It's a chance to explore where you're living in alignment with your true self and where you might be hiding behind a role that no longer serves you.

Exercise: Identify Three Roles You Regularly Play

Grab your journal, notebook, or a blank page, and take a few moments to reflect on the roles you play in your life.

Write down at least three roles that you regularly embody—roles that you find yourself stepping into day after day, whether at work, at home, or in your social circles.

Here are some examples to guide you:

- **The Professional Role**: Are you the one who is always put together, always competent, always ready to take charge? Do you feel like you can never show weakness or ask for help, even when you're overwhelmed?
- **The Caregiver Role**: Are you the one who takes care of everyone else's needs before your own? The person who is always there to support others, even when it means neglecting your own well-being?
- **The Achiever Role**: Are you the one who is always striving for more? The one who can't rest until you've accomplished the next goal, yet still feels like it's never quite enough?
- **The Peacemaker Role**: Are you the one who smooths over conflict, avoids confrontation, and keeps things harmonious, even at the expense of your own feelings or boundaries?
- **The "Good" Person Role**: Are you the one who always does the right thing, always meets expectations, always follows the rules, even when it means sacrificing your own desires or dreams?

Step 1: List the Three Roles

Once you've written down three roles, take a moment to reflect on how often you step into these roles.

Do they dominate your day-to-day life? Do they feel like second nature, or do they require effort? Are they roles you've chosen, or are they roles that have been placed upon you?

Step 2: Reflect on Each Role's Alignment with Your True Self

Now, for each role, ask yourself the following questions:

- **Do I feel authentic in this role?**
  Do I feel like myself when I'm in this role, or do I feel like I'm acting or performing to meet someone else's expectations?
- **Does this role energize or drain me?**
  After stepping into this role, do I feel fulfilled and energized, or do I feel exhausted and depleted? Authentic roles tend to energize us, while inauthentic ones often drain our energy.
- **Am I hiding parts of myself in this role?**
  Are there aspects of my personality, emotions, or desires that I'm suppressing in this role? Am I afraid to show certain sides of myself for fear of being judged, rejected, or misunderstood?
- **What would it feel like to live this role more authentically?**
  How could I bring more of my true self into this role? What masks could I start to let go of, even in small ways?

Step 3: Summarize Your Findings

After reflecting on each role, write a brief summary of your thoughts.

Did you notice that some roles feel more aligned with your true self than others? Were there any surprises or moments of clarity in what you uncovered? Do certain roles feel more like masks, while others feel more authentic?

Reflection on the Exercise

This exercise may bring up a lot of emotions—perhaps relief, as you recognize where you've been living authentically, or perhaps discomfort, as you see the masks you've been wearing for too long. Both experiences are valid.

The goal here is not to pass judgment on yourself but to simply observe where you are. Awareness is the first step toward meaningful change.

If you found that certain roles feel draining or inauthentic, that's okay. Recognizing that is a powerful step forward. It doesn't mean you have to abandon those roles overnight, but it does mean you have the opportunity to start bringing more of your true self into them.

Maybe it's as simple as speaking up more in your professional role or asserting your needs in your caregiving role. Small shifts can create profound changes over time.

If you found that some roles feel deeply aligned with your true self, celebrate that!

These are the parts of your life where you are living in integrity, where your actions and values are in harmony. These roles are where your true self shines through, and they're a source of strength.

Takeaway

Today, you've taken an important step in understanding how the roles you play shape your sense of self. Some roles may align beautifully with who you are, while others may feel more like masks that hide your true self. Both realities are part of the journey.

As we continue this 21-day journey, you'll begin to see that you don't have to abandon the roles that matter to you. Instead, you can start to bring more of your authentic self into each role, peeling back the layers of expectation and allowing your true self to shine through.

Tomorrow, we'll dive deeper into your personal story—the narrative you've created about who you are and how that story has shaped your life.

But for today, take a moment to acknowledge the insight you've gained. You're beginning to understand where you are living in alignment and where you're ready for change. You're stepping closer to living a life that feels true, empowered, and aligned with your authentic self.

Remember: You are more than the roles you play, and you deserve to live as the truest version of yourself. You are enough, just as you are.

DAY 3: REWRITING YOUR PERSONAL STORY

Welcome to Day 3. So far on this journey, you've started to meet your true self—the person beneath the roles, the masks, and the expectations of everyday life. You've taken a closer look at the different roles you play and begun to understand where you've been living in alignment with your authentic self and where you've been hiding behind the masks you wear.

Today, we're taking another powerful step forward by exploring something even deeper: *the stories you tell yourself and how they've shaped your self-identity*.

You may not realize it, but your personal narrative—the story you tell yourself about who you are, where you come from, and what you're capable of—has a profound impact on your life. It influences how you see yourself, how you interact with the world, and how you approach challenges and opportunities.

Our personal stories can either empower us or hold us back, depending on how we choose to frame them.

Today is about reclaiming your narrative and reshaping it in a way that reflects your resilience, your potential, and your true self.

The Power of Personal Narratives

Every one of us carries a story about ourselves. It's like an internal script we follow, often without even realizing it.

This script is built over time, shaped by our experiences, the people around us, and the beliefs we've internalized about ourselves. These stories start early in life.

From childhood, we begin to craft narratives about who we are based on the messages we receive from our families, friends, schools, and society at large.

Sometimes, these stories are positive and affirming. For example, you might tell yourself the story, "I am strong and capable of overcoming challenges."

That story becomes a source of inner strength and resilience. It helps you move forward, even when life gets difficult.

But just as often, we carry stories that limit us—stories that make us feel small, unworthy, or incapable. You might tell yourself, "I'm not good enough," or "I always fail when I try something new," or "I'm too damaged to be loved."

These stories can become like invisible chains, binding you to a version of yourself that isn't reflective of who you really are. They hold you back from growth, from taking risks, from believing in your potential.

Think of your personal story as a lens through which you view the world. If that lens is cloudy or distorted, everything you experience gets filtered through it. If you're carrying the belief that you're "not enough," then every setback or criticism becomes proof that the story is true. Even when something good happens, you might dismiss it or feel like you don't deserve it.

It's easy to become trapped in these limiting narratives, but the good news is this: *you have the power to rewrite your story.*

Today is about examining the stories you've been telling yourself—both the ones that empower you and the ones that hold you back.

It's about recognizing that while your past experiences have shaped your narrative, *you are the author of your story*, and you have the ability to reclaim that narrative in a way that serves you.

The Stories That Shape Us

Take a moment to reflect on the stories you've carried with you throughout your life.

Some of these stories may be deeply ingrained, passed down from family, or reinforced by experiences you've had over the years. Others might be more recent, formed by specific events or challenges.

Either way, they shape how you see yourself and how you move through the world.

For example, you might have a story about your childhood that centers around struggle. Maybe you grew up feeling unseen or undervalued, and that experience led you to believe that you're not worthy of attention or love.

Over time, that belief became a central part of your narrative. You might even see it playing out in your adult life—maybe you find it hard to ask for what you need in relationships, or you settle for less than you deserve because you've internalized the idea that your needs aren't important.

Or perhaps you've told yourself a story about failure. Maybe you tried something in the past—starting a business, pursuing a passion, or building a relationship—and it didn't work out the way you hoped.

That experience left you with the belief that you're "not capable" or that success is out of reach for you. Now, every time an opportunity arises, you hesitate or talk yourself out of it because you're carrying the story that "I always fail."

These stories may have been useful at some point. They might have helped you make sense of a difficult situation or protected you from disappointment.

But if they're still shaping your life in ways that limit your potential, it's time to rewrite them.

Why Rewriting Your Story Matters

When you hold onto a story that no longer serves you, you're essentially living in the past. You're allowing old beliefs, fears, and experiences to dictate your present and future.

Rewriting your story is about reclaiming your power. It's about taking ownership of your narrative and reshaping it in a way that reflects your growth, your strength, and your capacity for change.

This doesn't mean denying the difficult experiences you've had. It's not about pretending that everything has been easy or that you've never faced challenges.

Instead, it's about reframing those experiences in a way that honors your resilience and allows you to move forward with a sense of possibility.

For example, instead of carrying the story "I always fail," you might reframe it as, "I've faced challenges in the past, and each one has taught me valuable lessons. I am capable of learning and growing from every experience, and I am ready to succeed in new ways."

This new story acknowledges the reality of your past but shifts the focus from failure to growth. It empowers you to see yourself as capable and resilient, rather than stuck in a pattern of defeat.

Rewriting your story is one of the most powerful steps you can take on the journey to self-connection.

It allows you to let go of old narratives that have been holding you back and to step into a new version of yourself—one that is grounded in truth, possibility, and self-compassion.

Exercise: Journal Your Life Story, Focusing on Pivotal Moments

Today's exercise is an opportunity to reflect on your life story and identify the moments that have shaped you.

It's a chance to examine the narrative you've created about who you are and to begin the process of rewriting it in a way that reflects your true self.

Step 1: Write Your Life Story

Take out your journal or a blank piece of paper and begin to write your life story. Don't worry about making it perfect—this is not about creating a polished narrative.

Instead, focus on the key moments and experiences that have shaped who you are today.

Start by thinking about pivotal moments in your life—moments that stand out when you think about your journey.

These might be moments of challenge, change, joy, or pain. They could be related to your family, friendships, career, or personal growth.

As you write, allow yourself to reflect on how these moments have influenced your beliefs about yourself and the world.

Here are some prompts to guide you:

- **What were the defining moments in your childhood that shaped your sense of self?**

    Did you feel supported and valued, or did you struggle with feeling unseen or misunderstood? How did those early experiences shape the stories you've told yourself about your worth and capabilities?

- **What have been the key challenges or setbacks in your life?**

  How did those experiences impact your beliefs about yourself? Did they lead you to develop a story about being "not good enough" or "unworthy of success"?

- **What moments have brought you joy, accomplishment, or growth?**

  Do you allow yourself to fully embrace and celebrate these experiences, or do they get overshadowed by negative narratives? How have these positive moments contributed to your sense of self?

Let your thoughts flow freely as you write. The goal is to get everything out on the page so you can see your story laid out in front of you.

Step 2: Identify One Story You Want to Rewrite

After you've journaled your life story, take a moment to reflect on the narrative you've created. Look for any recurring themes or patterns. Pay attention to the stories that feel limiting or disempowering—stories that no longer serve you.

Ask yourself:

- **What's one story I've been telling myself that I'm ready to let go of?**
  This might be a story about your worth, your relationships, or your capabilities. It could be a belief that you're "not good enough," that you "always fail," or that you're "too damaged to be loved."
- **How has this story shaped my life?**
  Reflect on how this narrative has influenced your decisions, your relationships, and your sense of self. How has it held

you back from fully embracing your potential?

- **What new story can I create that reflects my growth and resilience?**
  Think about how you can rewrite this story in a way that honors your past but also opens up new possibilities for your future. Your new story should be grounded in self-compassion, empowerment, and a sense of possibility.

For example, if your current story is, "I'm not worthy of love because I've been hurt in the past," your new story might be, "I've learned valuable lessons from my past relationships, and I am worthy of love, connection, and joy."

This new narrative shifts the focus from pain to growth and opens the door to new experiences.

Step 3: Write Your New Story

Once you've identified the story you want to rewrite, take some time to craft your new narrative. Write it out in a way that feels empowering and aligned with your true self.

This new story should reflect not only your past experiences but also your strengths, your resilience, and the person you're becoming.

As you write, focus on the possibilities that exist for you now. Think about how this new story can guide your future decisions, actions, and beliefs.

Reflection on the Exercise

Rewriting your personal story is one of the most transformative steps you can take toward self-connection.

By examining the narratives you've been carrying, you've brought awareness to the beliefs that have shaped your life.

And by rewriting those stories, you've chosen to reclaim your power and live from a place of possibility, not limitation.

This new story is yours to carry forward. It's a living, breathing narrative that can continue to evolve as you grow. Keep it close and remind yourself of it often—especially in moments of doubt or fear.

This is your story, and you have the power to tell it in a way that reflects your true self.

Takeaway

Today, you made the powerful choice to reclaim your personal narrative. You recognized the stories that have been holding you back and took the courageous step of rewriting them in a way that reflects your resilience, strength, and capacity for growth.

Tomorrow, we'll explore the role of self-awareness and mindfulness in deepening your connection with yourself and staying grounded in your new story.

But for today, take a moment to celebrate the work you've done.

You are the author of your life, and you have the power to write a story that reflects the beauty, strength, and possibility of your true self.

Remember: Your story is yours to tell. Make it one that empowers you, honors your growth, and reflects the fullness of who you truly are.

You are enough, just as you are, and your story is just beginning.

DAY 4: THE POWER OF SELF-AWARENESS

Welcome to Day 4 of your journey. You've already done significant work in reconnecting with your true self. You've explored the roles and masks you wear, examined the stories you tell yourself, and even begun to rewrite those stories in a way that reflects your growth, resilience, and authenticity.

Today, we'll be taking an essential step forward: *the practice of self-awareness.*

Self-awareness is one of the most powerful tools you have in your journey to self-connection. It is the key to understanding your thoughts, emotions, reactions, and behaviors as they unfold in real time.

When you're self-aware, you're not just going through the motions of life on autopilot—you're living consciously, noticing how you feel, how you respond, and where your actions align (or don't align) with your true self.

This is where real change begins. Because once you become aware of your inner world, you can make choices that support your growth and well-being, rather than being controlled by unconscious patterns or habits.

Today's focus is on helping you cultivate this awareness through the practice of mindfulness.

By learning to observe your thoughts and emotions without judgment, you'll create the space needed to respond to life with intention and clarity.

What is Self-Awareness?

Self-awareness is about paying attention to what's happening *inside* you. It's about tuning in to your internal dialogue, your emotions, and even the physical sensations in your body, so you can understand how you're experiencing the present moment.

When you become aware of your thoughts and feelings, you begin to see patterns—patterns in how you react to stress, how you deal with disappointment, how you handle joy or success, and how you relate to others.

Think of self-awareness as shining a light on your inner world. Often, we move through life without really noticing what's going on inside us. We're consumed by external pressures—work, relationships, social obligations—so much so that we rarely stop to ask ourselves, *How do I really feel in this moment?* or *What am I thinking right now, and how is that affecting my actions?* Without that awareness, it's easy to be swept up in habits and behaviors that don't serve us.

For example, have you ever caught yourself reacting emotionally in a situation, only to realize later that your reaction had little to do with what was actually happening? Maybe you snapped at someone because you were already feeling stressed about something else. Or perhaps you found yourself retreating or withdrawing because old fears or insecurities got triggered.

These are moments when unconscious patterns take over. But with self-awareness, you can catch those patterns *in the moment* and make different choices—choices that are aligned with your true self.

The Benefits of Self-Awareness

So why is self-awareness so important? Because it gives you the power to change your relationship with yourself and the world around you. Here's what self-awareness can do for you:

1. **Empower You to Make Conscious Choices**: When you're self-aware, you can see the thought patterns or emotions driving your actions. Instead of reacting impulsively, you have the ability to pause, reflect, and choose a response that's more in line with your values and who you truly are.
2. **Increase Emotional Resilience**: Self-awareness helps you notice emotions as they arise, rather than being swept away by them. It allows you to acknowledge what you're feeling—whether it's frustration, sadness, anxiety, or joy—without letting those emotions control you. This ability to step back from your emotions gives you greater emotional strength and stability.
3. **Improve Relationships**: When you're aware of your inner state, you're better able to communicate how you feel and why you're reacting a certain way. This can improve your relationships, as you're more likely to approach situations from a place of honesty and self-understanding rather than defensiveness or reactivity.
4. **Strengthen Your Connection to Your True Self**: Self-awareness brings you back to the present moment, where your true self lives. It helps you notice when you're acting out of alignment with your values, so you can course-correct and make choices that feel authentic. Over time, self-awareness deepens your sense of self-connection and helps you live more fully in alignment with who you really are.

Mindfulness: The Gateway to Self-Awareness

One of the most effective ways to cultivate self-awareness is through the practice of mindfulness. Mindfulness is the act of being fully present in the moment, observing your thoughts, emotions, and sensations without judgment. When you practice mindfulness, you develop the ability to *notice* what's happening inside you without getting caught up in it.

For example, let's say you're feeling stressed. Instead of being swept away by that stress and letting it affect your mood or behavior, mindfulness allows you to take a step back and observe: *I'm feeling stressed right now. I notice that my breathing is shallow, my thoughts are racing, and my shoulders are tense.*

This simple act of observation creates space between you and the emotion, giving you the chance to respond more intentionally.

Mindfulness also teaches you to accept whatever is happening in the present moment, rather than trying to change or resist it. If you're feeling anxious, mindfulness allows you to notice that feeling without judging yourself for it. You simply observe it, knowing that it's a temporary state that will pass.

Over time, this practice helps you develop a more compassionate relationship with yourself and your emotions, because you're no longer fighting against them—you're simply observing and allowing them to be.

Common Challenges with Self-Awareness

Before we dive into today's exercise, it's important to acknowledge that self-awareness isn't always easy. Many people find it uncomfortable at first to sit with their thoughts and emotions. It can feel unsettling to notice what's really going on inside, especially if you're used to distracting yourself or avoiding difficult feelings.

You might find that when you start to pay attention, old fears or anxieties come up. Or you might discover that you've been carrying stress or tension in your body that you weren't even aware of. These realizations can be challenging, but they're also incredibly valuable. They give you insight into what's been happening beneath the surface and open the door to deeper healing and growth.

Remember, self-awareness is a *practice*. It's something you develop over time, and it requires patience and compassion. You don't have to be perfect at it.

The goal is simply to start noticing—without judgment—what's happening in your mind, body, and emotions. The more you practice, the easier it will become.

Exercise: 10-Minute Mindfulness Practice

Today's exercise is a simple mindfulness technique that will help you observe your thoughts and emotions without judgment.

The goal is to spend 10 minutes in a state of mindful awareness, noticing whatever arises in your mind and body without trying to control or change it.

This practice will help you develop the self-awareness needed to live more consciously and make choices that are in alignment with your true self.

Step 1: Find a Quiet Space

Begin by finding a quiet space where you won't be disturbed for the next 10 minutes. Sit in a comfortable position, either in a chair or on the floor with your legs crossed. Let your hands rest gently in your lap or on your knees. Close your eyes or lower your gaze.

Step 2: Focus on Your Breath

Start by bringing your attention to your breath. Notice the natural rhythm of your breathing as air flows in and out of your body. You don't need to change your breath—just observe it as it is. Feel the rise and fall of your chest or the sensation of air moving in and out of your nostrils.

Spend a minute or two grounding yourself in this awareness of your breath. This is your anchor to the present moment.

Step 3: Observe Your Thoughts

Now, gently shift your focus to your thoughts. As you sit in silence, you'll likely notice thoughts beginning to arise. It's completely natural for your mind to be active, so don't try to stop or control your thoughts. Instead, imagine that you're an observer—watching your thoughts as they pass by.

Some thoughts might be about your day, worries, plans for the future, or memories from the past. Whatever comes up, simply observe it without getting caught up in it. Let the thoughts come and go, like clouds passing across the sky.

If you find yourself getting lost in a thought or pulled into a mental story, gently bring your attention back to your breath.

It's normal for the mind to wander—just return to observing whenever you notice you've been distracted.

Step 4: Notice Emotions and Sensations

As you continue to sit in mindfulness, you may also notice emotions or physical sensations arising. Perhaps you feel a sense of calm, or maybe you're aware of tension in your body. You might notice feelings of anxiety, sadness, or restlessness.

Whatever arises, simply observe it with curiosity. Allow the emotion or sensation to be there without judging it or trying to change it.

Notice how it feels in your body. Is it warm or cool? Heavy or light? Does it move, or does it feel stuck?

Remember, your goal is not to fix or avoid anything—it's to *observe* with compassion. You're simply noticing what's present.

Step 5: End with Gratitude

After 10 minutes, slowly bring your awareness back to your breath. Take a few deep, grounding breaths, and allow yourself to feel a sense of gratitude for the time you've spent cultivating self-awareness.

When you're ready, gently open your eyes and return to the present moment.

Reflection on the Exercise

How did it feel to observe your thoughts and emotions without judgment? Did you notice any recurring themes or patterns in your thinking? Were there moments of peace, restlessness, or distraction?

If you found it challenging to stay focused or if difficult emotions came up, that's okay. Mindfulness is a practice, and it takes time to develop the ability to sit with your thoughts and feelings without being pulled into them.

The fact that you showed up and practiced today is a victory in itself.

Over time, this practice will help you build greater self-awareness. You'll start to notice patterns in your thinking and emotional responses, which will allow you to catch yourself in moments of unconscious reactivity.

This awareness is the foundation for making conscious, intentional choices that align with your true self.

Takeaway

Today, you took a powerful step toward cultivating self-awareness through mindfulness. By observing your thoughts and emotions without judgment, you began the process of creating space between stimulus and response—space that allows you to choose how you want to show up in each moment.

As you move forward, continue to practice mindfulness throughout your day. Notice when your mind begins to wander or when emotions arise, and gently bring your awareness back to the present moment.

The more you practice, the more connected you'll feel to your true self and the more empowered you'll be to live consciously.

Tomorrow, we'll explore the process of discovering your core values, which is an essential step in living a life that feels aligned and authentic.

But for now, take a moment to appreciate the self-awareness you've cultivated today. You're learning to live with greater intention, presence, and alignment—and that's a beautiful step toward becoming the truest version of yourself.

Remember: *Self-awareness is the foundation of growth, and you have the power to develop it one mindful moment at a time.*

DAY 5: DISCOVERING YOUR CORE VALUES

Welcome to Day 5. So far, your journey has been filled with meaningful reflection—meeting your true self, understanding the roles and masks you wear, rewriting your personal story, and cultivating self-awareness through mindfulness.

Today, we're going to dive into something that forms the bedrock of your authentic self: *your core values.*

Core values are the deeply held beliefs that shape who you are. They influence the choices you make, the relationships you build, and how you respond to the challenges and opportunities that life presents.

When you live in alignment with your values, you experience a sense of inner peace, purpose, and fulfillment. When you stray from them—whether because of external pressures, fear, or uncertainty—you can feel disconnected, restless, or stuck.

This process of uncovering and embracing your core values is about more than just listing traits you admire. It's about digging deep into the essence of what truly matters to you, identifying the principles that make you feel most alive and connected to your true self.

When you have a clear understanding of your core values, you have a guiding compass to help you navigate life's complexities with integrity and authenticity.

Today's focus is on helping you discover and articulate your top five core values.

By the end of this day, you'll not only have clarity about what truly drives you, but you'll also understand how these values shape your decisions, behaviors, and relationships—and how living in alignment with them can transform your life.

The Importance of Core Values

Your core values are not just abstract ideals—they are the foundation of your identity and the blueprint for how you live your life.

These values influence everything from the way you approach your career, to how you cultivate relationships, to the decisions you make about your personal growth. When you're clear about your values, you're empowered to make choices that are in alignment with your authentic self, and you become less susceptible to being swayed by external expectations or societal pressures.

But the challenge is that many of us don't consciously think about our values on a daily basis. We might have a vague sense of what matters to us—like family, honesty, or kindness—but we haven't taken the time to really define those values or reflect on how they show up in our lives.

When we're not clear about our values, it's easy to find ourselves making decisions that don't truly resonate with who we are. We may say yes to things that don't align with our priorities or find ourselves in situations that feel off, but we can't quite figure out why.

On the other hand, when you're crystal clear about your core values, they act as a filter for your decisions and actions. You can more easily say "yes" to opportunities and relationships that align with those values and confidently say "no" to anything that doesn't. You begin to live from a place of alignment and authenticity, rather than simply reacting to life's demands.

For example, if one of your core values is *family*, you might prioritize spending time with your loved ones over taking on extra work commitments. If *personal growth* is a core value, you might invest more time in learning and self-development, even if it means stepping out of your comfort zone.

When you live according to your values, your life begins to feel more intentional, fulfilling, and meaningful.

The Connection Between Core Values and Self-Connection

Core values are more than just guiding principles—they are a direct expression of your authentic self. Living in alignment with your values is what keeps you connected to who you truly are. They ground you in your truth and give you the clarity you need to navigate the world with confidence.

When you're disconnected from your values, it's easy to feel lost or adrift. You might find yourself going through the motions, making decisions based on what you think you *should* do rather than what actually feels right for you.

This disconnection can lead to feelings of dissatisfaction, confusion, or even burnout, because you're not living in alignment with what truly matters to you.

But when you're in touch with your values, you're able to live with purpose and integrity. You know what's important to you, and you're willing to make choices—even difficult ones—that honor those values.

This is the essence of self-connection: living a life that reflects who you truly are, rather than who others expect you to be.

By identifying your core values today, you'll be laying the foundation for deeper self-connection and more intentional living.

These values will become a touchstone for you as you continue to grow, evolve, and make decisions that align with your highest self.

Discovering Your Core Values: A Journey Inward

Uncovering your core values is a deeply personal process. It requires you to pause, reflect, and ask yourself what truly matters in your life—not just on a surface level, but at the deepest part of your being.

This exercise isn't about finding the "right" values or trying to impress anyone with your choices. It's about being honest with yourself and identifying the principles that resonate with your soul.

As we move through this process, I encourage you to embrace curiosity and openness. Allow yourself to explore without judgment or pressure. There's no rush, and there's no "right" answer.

The goal is to get in touch with the values that make you feel most alive and most connected to your authentic self.

Exercise: Discover Your Core Values

Today's exercise will help you identify your top five core values. These are the values that serve as the foundation for how you live your life—the principles that guide your decisions, shape your behavior, and define your sense of purpose.

Step 1: Reflect on Meaningful Moments in Your Life

Before identifying your core values, take a moment to reflect on the times in your life when you felt most aligned with yourself. These might be moments of joy, fulfillment, or personal achievement. They could also be times when you faced a challenge and came out stronger, realizing what truly mattered to you.

Some reflection prompts to guide you:

- **When have I felt most alive, fulfilled, or connected to myself?**
  What was happening in those moments? What values were present that made you feel that way? Was it a sense of *adventure, compassion, creativity,* or *integrity*?
- **What has been a pivotal moment of growth or change for me?**
  Think about a time when you had to make a difficult decision or overcome a challenge. What values did you lean on to guide you through that experience? Did you find strength in *resilience, courage,* or *faith*?
- **What are the qualities I most admire in myself or others?**
  Consider the traits that you respect and aspire to embody. Do you value *honesty, kindness,* or *independence*? What do these qualities say about who you are and what's important to you?

As you reflect on these moments, start jotting down words or phrases that capture the values that were present.

Don't worry about getting it perfect—just let your thoughts flow and allow yourself to explore.

Step 2: Identify Your Top Five Core Values

Once you've reflected on the meaningful moments in your life, it's time to narrow down your list to your top five core values.

These are the values that feel most central to who you are—the ones that guide your choices, behaviors, and sense of purpose.

Here's a list of common core values to help inspire you:

- Integrity
- Compassion

- Courage
- Creativity
- Family
- Freedom
- Adventure
- Growth
- Balance
- Honesty
- Connection
- Kindness
- Service
- Spirituality
- Innovation
- Curiosity
- Trust
- Justice
- Self-Respect

As you look at this list, notice which words resonate with you. Don't overthink it—go with your gut. What values make you feel energized, inspired, and true to yourself?

Once you've identified your top five, write them down.

Step 3: Reflect on How These Values Guide Your Choices and Behaviors

Now that you've identified your core values, it's time to reflect on how these values show up in your life. How do they influence the decisions you make, the relationships you cultivate, and the way you spend your time?

Here are some prompts to guide your reflection:

- **How do my values influence my decisions?**
  Think about how your values have guided your past decisions—whether it's choosing a career path, deciding where to live, or navigating personal relationships. Do you feel like your choices are in alignment with your values, or

are there areas where you've compromised?
- **Are there areas of my life where I'm not living in alignment with my values?**
Consider any areas where you've strayed from your values—perhaps because of external pressures or fear. How does it feel to be out of alignment, and what steps can you take to reconnect with your values in those areas?
- **How can I use my values to guide future decisions?**
Moving forward, how can you use your core values as a compass to guide your actions? Whether it's making a big life decision or navigating day-to-day choices, how can your values help you stay true to yourself?

This reflection will help you gain clarity on how your core values shape your life and where you may need to make adjustments to live more authentically.

Reflection on the Exercise

How did it feel to identify your core values? Did any specific values surprise you, or did they affirm what you already knew about yourself?

This exercise is not only about discovering what matters most to you—it's about deepening your connection to your true self by aligning your life with your values.

Your core values are more than just words on a page—they are the foundation of who you are. They guide your decisions, help you set boundaries, and give you clarity in times of uncertainty. As you move forward, these values will serve as your inner compass, helping you navigate life with greater confidence and authenticity.

If you find that certain areas of your life are not in alignment with your values, that's okay. This awareness is an invitation to realign your life with what truly matters to you.

Remember, you have the power to make choices that honor your values, even if those choices feel difficult at times.

The more you live in alignment with your values, the more connected you'll feel to your authentic self—and the more fulfilling your life will become.

Takeaway

Today, you took a powerful step toward self-connection by discovering your core values. These values are the foundation of who you are and will guide you as you continue to grow and evolve.

By living in alignment with your values, you'll create a life that feels authentic, meaningful, and true to who you are.

As you move forward, let your core values guide your decisions, relationships, and actions. Whenever you feel uncertain or disconnected, return to these values as a source of clarity and grounding. They will remind you of who you are and what truly matters to you.

Tomorrow, we'll explore how embracing vulnerability can deepen your self-connection and help you build more authentic relationships.

But for today, take a moment to appreciate the clarity you've gained about what truly matters to you. You're not just living by default—you're living intentionally, with purpose and authenticity, guided by the principles that reflect your highest self.

Remember: *Your core values are the essence of who you are. Let them guide you as you create a life that reflects your true self.*

DAY 6: EMBRACING VULNERABILITY

Welcome to Day 6. So far on this journey, you've begun peeling back the layers of your true self—meeting the person beneath the roles and masks, identifying your core values, and practicing mindfulness to cultivate self-awareness.

Today, we're going to explore a key element of self-connection that often feels uncomfortable but is deeply transformative: *vulnerability*.

Vulnerability is the gateway to authentic living, both with yourself and with others. It's the act of allowing yourself to be seen, in all your humanity—imperfections, emotions, fears, and all.

For many of us, vulnerability can feel like standing on the edge of a cliff, unsure of what will happen if we leap. Will we be judged? Rejected? Misunderstood? But vulnerability is also the source of our deepest connections, our greatest moments of growth, and our ability to fully embrace who we are.

Without vulnerability, we cannot be fully present with ourselves or others. And in a world that often tells us to armor up, to hide behind perfection or control, learning to embrace vulnerability is an act of courage that leads to profound freedom.

Today is about stepping into that space of openness, learning to trust yourself enough to be emotionally honest, and understanding how vulnerability can transform your relationships and your life.

The Nature of Vulnerability

At its core, vulnerability is about emotional exposure. It's about showing parts of yourself that you might usually keep hidden—your fears, your insecurities, your doubts—because to be vulnerable is to be real.

Vulnerability is not about weakness; it's about *authenticity*. It's saying, "This is who I am," without the need for pretense or perfection.

We often view vulnerability through a lens of risk because it requires letting go of control. When we're vulnerable, we're not guaranteed a particular outcome—we don't know how others will respond, or even how we'll feel once we've opened up.

But this uncertainty is part of what makes vulnerability so powerful. It is in that uncertain space that real connection, growth, and change can happen.

It's also important to remember that vulnerability isn't just about sharing your struggles or challenges. It's also about sharing your joy, your hopes, and your dreams—things that can feel just as vulnerable, because admitting what we deeply desire or what brings us happiness can feel just as risky as sharing our fears.

We worry that if we share these things and they're not met with understanding, we'll be left feeling isolated or misunderstood.

But here's the truth: when you open yourself up, when you choose to be vulnerable, you allow others to see the real you, and you create the possibility for deeper, more meaningful connections.

You also create the opportunity for your own personal growth, because vulnerability allows you to face your fears and embrace your own humanity.

Why Vulnerability Is Essential for Self-Connection

Vulnerability is at the heart of self-connection because it allows you to be honest with yourself about your emotions, your needs, and your experiences. When you resist vulnerability, you're often resisting the truth of what's happening inside you. Maybe you avoid feeling sadness because it feels too heavy, or you suppress anger because you've been taught that it's "unacceptable." Perhaps you shy away from admitting that you need help because you want to appear strong and independent.

But avoiding vulnerability doesn't make those feelings go away—it simply buries them, creating distance between you and your true self.

The more you avoid vulnerability, the more disconnected you become from your emotions, and ultimately, from yourself.

When you allow yourself to be vulnerable, you're choosing to embrace the fullness of your human experience. You're saying, "I'm willing to feel all of it—joy, pain, fear, love—because that's what it means to be alive."

Vulnerability is what allows you to connect with the parts of yourself that need compassion, healing, and attention. It's also what makes space for you to celebrate your strengths, your resilience, and your growth.

By embracing vulnerability, you're giving yourself permission to be imperfect, to make mistakes, and to be a work in progress. You're also allowing yourself to experience the richness of life's emotional landscape. And in doing so, you build a deeper connection with your true self—one that's grounded in authenticity, rather than avoidance or fear.

Vulnerability and Relationships: The Power of Being Seen

Vulnerability doesn't just deepen your relationship with yourself—it also transforms your relationships with others. Think about the relationships in your life where you feel most connected, most understood, and most loved. Chances are, those relationships are built on a foundation of vulnerability.

When you allow yourself to be vulnerable with someone—whether it's a friend, partner, or family member—you're giving them the gift of your authentic self. You're saying, "Here I am, without the masks, without the defenses." In doing so, you create a space for them to show up authentically, too. This mutual vulnerability is what allows relationships to flourish. It fosters trust, intimacy, and a deep sense of connection.

But vulnerability in relationships can feel risky, because it opens the door to being hurt. When we let someone see our fears, our insecurities, or our dreams, we run the risk that they might not understand or accept us. Yet it's precisely this risk that makes vulnerability so powerful.

By being emotionally open, you give yourself the chance to experience the fullness of connection—the kind of connection that's built on real understanding and empathy, rather than surface-level interactions.

It's also important to remember that vulnerability in relationships isn't about oversharing or exposing yourself in ways that don't feel safe.

Vulnerability is about being intentional with your emotional openness, sharing what feels true and necessary, and building trust over time.

Overcoming the Fear

of Vulnerability

The fear of vulnerability is universal. It's rooted in the fear of rejection, judgment, or the possibility of being hurt. We all have moments where we think, *"What if I open up and they don't understand?"* or *"What if I show my real self and I'm not accepted?"*

These fears can keep us locked in a state of emotional protection, where we hide parts of ourselves to avoid feeling exposed.

But here's the thing: when you armor up against vulnerability, you're not just protecting yourself from potential hurt—you're also shutting yourself off from joy, connection, and love. The walls you build to keep pain out also keep connection from getting in. And over time, those walls can leave you feeling isolated and disconnected—not only from others, but from your own emotional truth.

So, how do you overcome the fear of vulnerability? It starts with trust—trusting yourself and trusting the process. Trust that you are resilient enough to handle the discomfort that vulnerability brings. Trust that even if you're misunderstood or judged, you are still worthy of love and connection. And trust that being vulnerable is not a sign of weakness—it's an act of strength and courage.

The Freedom of Vulnerability

One of the most beautiful things about vulnerability is the freedom it brings. When you allow yourself to be emotionally open, you free yourself from the pressure of perfection. You stop trying to be who you think others want you to be, and you start living as your true self.

Vulnerability also frees you from the need to control everything. It teaches you to let go of the outcome and simply trust that showing up authentically is enough. When you embrace vulnerability, you're no longer hiding behind defenses or trying to protect yourself from every possible hurt. Instead, you're allowing life to unfold naturally, knowing that whatever happens, you'll be okay.

This freedom is transformative because it allows you to step into your power. You begin to see that your worth isn't tied to how perfectly you manage your emotions or how flawlessly you present yourself to the world.

Your worth comes from your authenticity—from your willingness to show up as you are, with all your imperfections and strengths.

Exercise: Reflect on a Time You Were Vulnerable

Today's exercise is about reflecting on a time when you allowed yourself to be vulnerable. By revisiting this moment, you can gain insight into what vulnerability taught you and how it shaped your growth.

This reflection will help you deepen your understanding of how vulnerability has impacted your life and how it can continue to serve you moving forward.

Step 1: Recall a Time You Were Vulnerable

Think back to a time when you allowed yourself to be emotionally open and vulnerable.

This could be a conversation with a loved one where you expressed your true feelings, a moment when you admitted a mistake or asked for help, or a time when you shared something deeply personal. It could also be an internal moment when you acknowledged something difficult within yourself.

Consider the following prompts to guide your reflection:

- **What made this situation feel vulnerable for you?**
  Were you afraid of being judged, rejected, or

misunderstood? Reflect on what made this moment feel emotionally risky.

- **How did you feel in the moment?**
  Did you feel nervous, exposed, or uncertain? Did you also feel a sense of relief or authenticity by being open?

Step 2: Reflect on What You Learned

Now, reflect on what you gained from that experience of vulnerability. Did it deepen your connection with someone else? Did it teach you something about yourself? Did it lead to a sense of growth or healing?

Some prompts to guide your reflection:

- **How did others respond to your vulnerability?**
  Were you met with empathy, understanding, or support? Or did the experience challenge your expectations of how vulnerability would be received?
- **What did this experience teach you about the power of vulnerability?**
  Reflect on how this experience shifted your perspective on emotional openness. Did it help you develop more courage, self-compassion, or authenticity?

Step 3: Integrate the Lessons of Vulnerability

After reflecting on your past experience, think about how you can continue to embrace vulnerability moving forward. How can you be more open in your relationships? How can you practice emotional honesty with yourself? Where in your life could you let go of the need for perfection and lean into vulnerability?

Consider these prompts for moving forward:

- **How can I be more vulnerable in my daily life?**
  Are there areas where you've been holding back emotionally? How might you begin to open up, even in small ways, to build deeper connections with yourself and

others?
- **What fears do I need to overcome to embrace vulnerability?**
Are there specific fears—such as fear of rejection, failure, or judgment—that hold you back? How can you begin to release those fears and step into emotional openness?

Reflection on the Exercise

How did it feel to reflect on your experience of vulnerability? What emotions came up as you revisited that moment? Did you notice any patterns in how you approach vulnerability—either a willingness to be open or a tendency to protect yourself?

Vulnerability is challenging, but it's also one of the most powerful tools for personal growth and connection.

By reflecting on your past experiences, you've gained insight into the ways vulnerability has shaped your life—and the potential it holds for deepening your self-connection.

Takeaway

Today, you took a courageous step by reflecting on vulnerability—a cornerstone of authentic living. You've explored the role vulnerability plays in your life, how it has impacted your relationships, and how it can help you build deeper connections with yourself and others.

As you move forward, continue to practice vulnerability in your daily life. Allow yourself to be emotionally open, even when it feels uncomfortable.

The more you embrace vulnerability, the more connected you'll feel to your true self—and the more authentic and fulfilling your relationships will become.

Tomorrow, we'll explore the practice of cultivating self-compassion, another vital element of self-connection.

But for today, take a moment to honor the bravery it takes to be vulnerable. You're learning to live more fully and authentically, and that's a powerful step toward becoming the truest version of yourself.

Remember: *Vulnerability is the pathway to connection, authenticity, and freedom. When you show up as you truly are, you create space for deeper, more meaningful relationships with yourself and others.*

DAY 7: EXPANDING YOUR EMOTIONAL VOCABULARY

Welcome to Day 7 of your journey. You've spent the past week uncovering layers of your true self—understanding the roles you play, rewriting your personal stories, embracing vulnerability, and identifying your core values.

Today, we'll focus on one of the most powerful ways to deepen self-awareness and emotional intelligence: *expanding your emotional vocabulary*.

Your emotional vocabulary is the range of words you use to describe your feelings. Being able to accurately name and describe your emotions is essential for self-connection because it helps you make sense of what you're experiencing on a deeper level. When you can put words to your feelings, you unlock the power to understand, process, and express them with greater clarity. And in doing so, you cultivate a more nuanced relationship with yourself and those around you.

For many, emotional vocabulary is limited to a handful of words like "happy," "sad," "angry," or "stressed." But emotions are far more complex and varied than these basic terms allow.

By expanding your emotional vocabulary, you gain a richer, more accurate understanding of your inner world. It's like switching from seeing the world in black and white to experiencing the full spectrum of colors.

Today, we'll explore why expanding your emotional vocabulary is essential for emotional intelligence, how it can improve your relationships, and how to start building a more nuanced emotional lexicon that truly reflects your experience.

Why Expanding Your Emotional Vocabulary Matters

Imagine trying to describe a sunset with only three colors: red, blue, and green. It would be nearly impossible to capture the beauty, subtlety, and depth of the moment.

The same is true for your emotions. If you're limited to just a few words, you can't fully articulate the complexity of what you're feeling.

When you expand your emotional vocabulary, you give yourself the ability to describe your emotions with more precision. Instead of simply saying "I'm sad," you might realize you're feeling "disappointed," "grieving," or "melancholy." Each of these words carries its own unique meaning and context, and by naming them accurately, you can better understand what your emotions are telling you.

Emotions are signals—they provide valuable information about your needs, desires, and boundaries. But to interpret those signals effectively, you need to name them with accuracy.

By developing a broader emotional vocabulary, you give yourself the ability to tune into those signals and respond in a way that honors your true self.

For example, if you can distinguish between feeling "irritated" versus feeling "resentful," you'll be better equipped to address the underlying cause of that emotion. Irritation might signal a temporary frustration, while resentment could point to deeper feelings of unfairness or unmet needs.

This kind of precision helps you navigate your inner world with more clarity and insight, which in turn allows you to make choices that are aligned with your well-being.

The Connection Between Emotional Vocabulary and Self-Connection

Emotions are a natural and essential part of your inner landscape. They give you clues about how you're experiencing the world, and when you can name them with specificity, you gain the power to understand yourself more deeply.

Think about a time when you've felt overwhelmed but couldn't quite pinpoint why. Maybe it was more than just "stress." Perhaps you were feeling "overloaded," "pressured," or even "uncertain." These subtle distinctions matter because each of those emotions points to a different underlying experience.

Being able to name those emotions accurately not only helps you understand them better but also enables you to take action in response.

Self-connection requires that you be present with your emotions—not just the big ones, like joy or anger, but the subtle, often overlooked emotions that color your day-to-day life. When you expand your emotional vocabulary, you become better equipped to notice and name those subtleties.

This gives you the power to check in with yourself more often, recognize when something feels off, and course-correct before small emotions snowball into larger issues.

In addition, having a rich emotional vocabulary helps you embrace the full range of your emotional experience. Life isn't just about feeling good or bad—it's about learning to navigate the wide spectrum of emotions in between.

By accurately naming your feelings, you honor their presence without rushing to label them as "good" or "bad." Instead, you allow yourself to experience the fullness of your emotions, knowing that each one has something to teach you.

Emotional Vocabulary and Relationships

Expanding your emotional vocabulary doesn't just benefit your relationship with yourself—it also improves your relationships with others.

Clear communication is the foundation of any healthy relationship, and that starts with being able to accurately express how you're feeling.

When you can describe your emotions in a nuanced way, you give others the opportunity to truly understand you. Instead of saying, "I'm fine" or "I'm upset," you might be able to say, "I'm feeling overwhelmed because I've been trying to balance too many things at once."

This level of detail not only helps others respond to you more empathetically, but it also fosters deeper emotional connection.

It also allows you to ask for what you need. If you can clearly articulate your feelings, you're more likely to know what kind of support you're seeking—whether it's space, a listening ear, or reassurance.

In moments of conflict, being able to name your emotions with specificity can diffuse tension by helping both you and the other person understand what's really at the heart of the issue.

For example, rather than saying, "I'm mad at you," you might say, "I'm feeling hurt because I felt dismissed in our conversation."

This doesn't just name the emotion; it provides context and clarity, which opens the door for productive dialogue.

How a Limited Emotional Vocabulary Holds You Back

A limited emotional vocabulary can keep you trapped in confusion, frustration, or emotional stagnation. When you don't have the words to describe what you're feeling, your emotions can remain unprocessed and misunderstood.

This often leads to frustration or emotional buildup because you don't fully understand what's going on inside you.

Think of emotional vocabulary like a toolkit. If you only have a hammer, every problem looks like a nail. But if you expand your toolkit to include wrenches, screwdrivers, and pliers, you can approach each challenge with the right tool.

Similarly, when you have a broader emotional vocabulary, you can approach your emotions with more insight and precision. You can name what's really going on, and as a result, you can deal with your emotions in a healthier, more constructive way.

Without the language to describe your emotions, you might find yourself defaulting to vague terms like "bad" or "fine," which don't give you much insight into what you're truly feeling.

And when you don't understand your emotions, it's difficult to know how to move forward—whether that's finding a solution, asking for help, or simply allowing yourself to sit with your feelings.

By expanding your emotional vocabulary, you unlock a greater capacity for self-awareness and emotional regulation. You gain the power to name, process, and move through your emotions, rather than being stuck in them.

Exercise: Create Your Emotional Vocabulary List

Today's exercise is designed to help you expand your emotional vocabulary so you can describe your feelings with greater precision and depth.

By building a richer emotional lexicon, you'll be better equipped to understand yourself and communicate more clearly with others.

Step 1: Build Your Emotional Vocabulary

Start by writing down some of the basic emotions you tend to experience most often. You might include common feelings like:

- Happy
- Sad
- Angry
- Anxious
- Excited
- Frustrated

Next, let's dive deeper. For each of these basic emotions, try to come up with more specific terms that capture different nuances of that feeling. Here are some examples to guide you:

- **Happy**: Joyful, content, fulfilled, grateful, peaceful, elated, proud, hopeful, inspired
- **Sad**: Disappointed, heartbroken, lonely, grieving, discouraged, nostalgic, melancholic, rejected
- **Angry**: Frustrated, irritable, resentful, betrayed, outraged, offended, powerless, bitter
- **Anxious**: Nervous, worried, overwhelmed, tense, uneasy, insecure, panicked, restless
- **Excited**: Enthusiastic, eager, energized, motivated, hopeful, exhilarated, optimistic
- **Frustrated**: Defeated, blocked, stuck, impatient, powerless, discouraged, irritated

Add any other emotions you've experienced recently. Reflect on times when you felt confused about how to describe your emotions—could any of these new terms help you articulate them more clearly?

Step 2: Reflect on Recent Emotions

Now that you've built your emotional vocabulary list, practice using these words to describe recent feelings. Reflect on the past few days or weeks. How have you been feeling? Use your expanded vocabulary to pinpoint your emotions more precisely.

Here are some prompts to guide your reflection:

- **How am I feeling right now?**
  Look at your emotional vocabulary list and choose the words that most accurately describe how you're feeling in this moment. Are you feeling "hopeful" or "energized"? Or perhaps "anxious" or "overwhelmed"?
- **What emotions have I experienced recently?**
  Think about a recent event that triggered strong emotions. Use your expanded vocabulary to name those feelings. Were you "frustrated" or "disappointed"? "Joyful" or "grateful"? Be as specific as possible.
- **What emotions do I tend to avoid naming?**
  Are there certain emotions you often overlook or struggle to articulate? How can you use your expanded vocabulary to bring more awareness to those feelings?

Step 3: Use Your Vocabulary in Conversations

The next step is to practice using these new emotional terms in your conversations. Whether you're talking to a friend, partner, or family member, try to describe your emotions with more precision.

For example, instead of saying, "I'm just feeling off," you might say, "I've been feeling a little restless and unsure about a decision I need to make." Notice how the conversation shifts when you use more specific terms to describe how you're feeling.

Here are some examples of how you can use your emotional

vocabulary in real-time:
- **In a personal reflection**: "I've been feeling a little disconnected lately, like I'm missing a deeper sense of fulfillment."
- **In a conversation**: "I'm feeling overwhelmed right now because there are so many responsibilities pulling me in different directions."
- **In conflict**: "I'm feeling hurt and frustrated because I didn't feel heard during our conversation."

By practicing this regularly, you'll become more comfortable expressing your emotions with clarity and depth, which can lead to stronger connections with others and a deeper understanding of yourself.

Reflection on the Exercise

How did it feel to expand your emotional vocabulary? Did you find it easier to name your emotions with more nuance? Were there any emotions that became clearer or more understandable through this practice?

As you continue to build your emotional vocabulary, you'll notice how it enhances your ability to process and express your feelings. You'll feel more connected to your inner world and more capable of navigating the full range of emotions with grace and self-awareness.

Takeaway

Today, you expanded your emotional vocabulary, opening up new ways to understand and express your feelings.

By learning to name your emotions with greater accuracy, you've deepened your self-awareness and built the tools needed for more authentic communication.

As you continue on this journey, keep practicing your emotional vocabulary—both in your internal reflections and in your conversations with others.

The more you use these new terms, the more fluent you'll become in navigating your emotions with clarity and compassion.

Tomorrow, we'll explore how to create space for your emotions and build emotional resilience. But for today, take a moment to appreciate the new insights you've gained about your emotional world. You're learning to honor and express your emotions with more precision, and that's a powerful step toward becoming your most authentic self.

Remember: *Emotions are not something to be fixed or avoided—they are to be understood and expressed with clarity. The more words you have for your feelings, the more deeply you can connect with yourself and others.*

PART 2: STRENGTHENING YOUR EMOTIONAL CORE

Week 2: Building Resilience and Self-Compassion

DAY 8: THE POWER OF SELF-COMPASSION

Welcome to Day 8. You've spent the past week exploring vulnerability, expanding your emotional vocabulary, and aligning with your true self. Now, we begin Week 2: *Building Resilience and Self-Compassion*—an essential part of emotional strength and well-being.

Today, we'll focus on a practice that is often overlooked but is vital for emotional resilience: *self-compassion*.

Self-compassion is a way of relating to yourself with kindness, especially in difficult moments. It's about learning to be your own ally instead of your own harshest critic.

Many of us are quick to offer compassion and understanding to others, but when it comes to ourselves, we can be unrelenting—holding ourselves to impossibly high standards and punishing ourselves for not meeting them.

But here's the truth: self-compassion doesn't make you weak or indulgent. It makes you *stronger*. It's the practice of acknowledging your struggles, mistakes, and imperfections with the same warmth and kindness you would extend to a close friend.

This practice helps you build resilience because it allows you to move through life's challenges with greater emotional balance and care.

Today, you'll learn how to practice self-compassion, especially in moments when you feel like you've fallen short or when life feels overwhelming.

You'll also experience firsthand the power of writing a compassionate letter to yourself—a practice that can transform your inner dialogue and help you build a deeper sense of inner support.

What Is Self-Compassion?

Self-compassion is the practice of treating yourself with the same kindness, understanding, and patience that you would offer to someone you care about. It involves three key elements:

1. **Self-Kindness**: Being warm and understanding toward yourself, especially when you're struggling, rather than being overly harsh or critical. Self-kindness means recognizing that you don't need to be perfect to be deserving of love and care.
2. **Common Humanity**: Recognizing that everyone makes mistakes, faces challenges, and experiences difficult emotions. You are not alone in your struggles. This understanding can help reduce feelings of isolation or shame, which often come from believing you're the only one going through something difficult.
3. **Mindfulness**: Being present with your emotions without suppressing or exaggerating them. Mindfulness allows you to acknowledge your pain without being consumed by it. It helps you hold space for your feelings without over-identifying with them.

When you practice self-compassion, you acknowledge your own suffering without judgment. You give yourself permission to feel what you're feeling and to treat yourself with care and respect. Instead of saying, "I should be able to handle this better," you might say, "This is really hard right now, and it's okay to struggle. I'm doing the best I can."

Why Self-Compassion Is Essential for Resilience

Resilience is your ability to recover from setbacks, adapt to change, and keep moving forward, even when life feels challenging.

But true resilience isn't about "toughing it out" or pushing through difficult emotions without acknowledging them. It's about learning how to support yourself emotionally so that you can navigate those challenges with grace and self-care.

This is where self-compassion comes in. When you practice self-compassion, you create an internal environment of safety and support. Instead of tearing yourself down for your mistakes or failures, you learn to meet yourself with empathy and understanding.

This kindness toward yourself builds emotional resilience because it helps you recover more quickly from setbacks.

Imagine going through a difficult period in your life—maybe you're struggling at work, feeling overwhelmed with personal responsibilities, or dealing with a relationship issue. In moments like these, it's easy to turn inward and be your own harshest critic. You might think, *"Why can't I handle this better?"* or *"I'm such a failure."*

But self-compassion shifts this inner dialogue. Instead of criticizing yourself, you acknowledge the difficulty of the situation and remind yourself that it's okay to struggle. You offer yourself the same kindness and encouragement you would give to someone you love.

This shift in perspective makes all the difference. It doesn't mean you won't face challenges—but it does mean that when challenges arise, you'll have the emotional strength to get through them without tearing yourself down in the process.

Overcoming Self-Criticism

For many of us, self-criticism feels like a default mode. We've been conditioned to believe that being hard on ourselves is the only way to improve or succeed. Maybe you've internalized the message that self-compassion is a sign of weakness or that you don't deserve kindness until you've "earned" it.

But the reality is that self-criticism rarely leads to growth. In fact, it often has the opposite effect—it makes you feel more defeated, more overwhelmed, and less capable of bouncing back from setbacks.

Self-compassion, on the other hand, creates a supportive environment for growth because it allows you to acknowledge your struggles without feeling ashamed or inadequate.

Consider this: When you make a mistake or face a challenge, does criticizing yourself make it easier to move forward? Or does it make you feel stuck and paralyzed? Self-compassion offers a different path.

By treating yourself with kindness, you create space for healing, learning, and moving forward. You begin to see that mistakes are part of the human experience, not a reflection of your worth.

Exercise: Write a Compassionate Letter to Yourself

Today's exercise will help you practice self-compassion by writing a compassionate letter to yourself.

This is a powerful way to shift your inner dialogue from one of criticism to one of kindness and understanding. Writing this letter will allow you to acknowledge your struggles, offer yourself empathy, and remind yourself that you are worthy of care and compassion.

Step 1: Reflect on a Recent Challenge

Before you begin writing, take a moment to think about a recent challenge or difficult experience you've faced. It could be something related to your work, relationships, or personal life. Choose a situation where you felt like you were struggling or where you've been hard on yourself.

Once you've identified the situation, reflect on how you've been treating yourself in response to this challenge. Have you been critical of yourself for not handling it "perfectly"? Have you felt overwhelmed by feelings of inadequacy or frustration? This is an opportunity to bring awareness to your self-talk.

Step 2: Write Your Compassionate Letter

Now, imagine that you are writing to a dear friend who is going through the same challenge. How would you speak to them? What words of encouragement, kindness, and empathy would you offer? Use that same compassionate voice to write a letter to yourself.

Begin by acknowledging the difficulty of the situation. Let yourself express how hard it has been and validate your feelings without judgment. You might write something like:

"Dear [Your Name],
I know that you've been going through a really tough time lately. This challenge you're facing feels overwhelming, and it's okay to feel the way you do. I see how much effort you're putting in, and I want to remind you that it's okay to struggle. You don't have to be perfect to be worthy of kindness—especially from yourself."

Next, offer yourself words of comfort and encouragement. Remind yourself that you're not alone in facing difficulties and that you're doing the best you can. You might include phrases like:

- *"It's okay to make mistakes. Everyone does."*

- *"You're doing your best, and that's enough."*
- *"You don't have to have it all figured out right now. It's okay to take things one step at a time."*
- *"I believe in your ability to get through this, even when it feels hard."*

As you write, focus on offering yourself the same warmth and understanding that you would extend to a close friend. Allow yourself to be compassionate, even if it feels uncomfortable at first.

Step 3: Read Your Letter Aloud

Once you've written your letter, take a moment to read it aloud to yourself. Let the words resonate with you. Notice how it feels to hear those words of kindness and encouragement directed toward you. Does it feel comforting? Does it feel unfamiliar? Allow yourself to receive the compassion you're offering, without judgment.

Reading your letter aloud can be a powerful way to internalize the message. You're not just writing for the sake of writing—you're creating an opportunity to connect with yourself in a deeper, more compassionate way.

Step 4: Reflect on the Experience

After reading your letter, take a few moments to reflect on how the experience felt. Did any parts of the letter resonate with you more than others? Did you notice any resistance or discomfort? Or did you feel a sense of relief in offering yourself kindness?

This exercise is about building a habit of self-compassion. The more you practice, the easier it will become to treat yourself with kindness in difficult moments.

Remember, self-compassion is not something you have to "earn." It's something you're worthy of simply because you are human.

Reflection on the Exercise

Writing a compassionate letter to yourself might feel unfamiliar at first, especially if you're used to being self-critical.

But self-compassion is a skill that grows with practice. The more you offer yourself kindness, the more natural it will become to treat yourself with care and understanding.

How did it feel to write this letter? Did you notice any shifts in your inner dialogue? Were there moments of discomfort, or did you find it freeing to offer yourself compassion?

This is the beginning of a powerful practice that can transform how you relate to yourself, especially in moments of struggle.

Takeaway

Today, you took a meaningful step toward building resilience by practicing self-compassion.

By writing a compassionate letter to yourself, you learned how to offer yourself the same kindness and understanding that you would extend to a close friend.

This practice will help you navigate difficult moments with greater emotional strength and balance.

As you continue on this journey, remember that self-compassion is not a luxury—it's a necessity. It's a way of supporting yourself through life's challenges, building resilience, and deepening your connection with your true self.

Tomorrow, we'll continue exploring emotional resilience by learning how to embrace discomfort as a pathway to growth.

But for today, take a moment to appreciate the kindness you've offered yourself. You are worthy of that kindness, and it will carry you through even the toughest times.

Remember: *Self-compassion is not self-indulgence. It's self-care. You are deserving of kindness, especially in your most difficult moments.*

DAY 9: SETTING HEALTHY BOUNDARIES

Welcome to Day 9. You've been doing important inner work—building self-compassion, practicing vulnerability, and connecting with your emotions.

Today's focus is a vital skill that will help you protect and sustain that connection with yourself: *setting healthy boundaries*.

Boundaries are essential for maintaining emotional energy, respecting your needs, and ensuring that your relationships are built on mutual respect. Without boundaries, it's easy to lose yourself in the demands of others, and eventually, you might find yourself feeling depleted, resentful, or disconnected from your true self.

Learning to set and enforce healthy boundaries is one of the most empowering acts of self-care you can give yourself.

Today, we'll explore why boundaries matter, how they're connected to your emotional well-being, and what steps you can take to identify where you need stronger boundaries in your life.

By the end of today, you'll have a clear sense of where your boundaries are needed and a practical plan for maintaining them.

Why Boundaries Are Vital for Your Well-Being

Boundaries are not barriers—they are *guidelines* that help define what is acceptable for you in your relationships, your work, and your daily life. They reflect what you need in order to feel respected, balanced, and emotionally safe.

When you set clear boundaries, you protect your emotional and mental well-being, ensuring that your needs are honored while still engaging with others from a place of generosity and respect.

However, when you allow your boundaries to be crossed—whether by overcommitting, allowing others to take advantage of your time, or putting others' needs before your own—you create a situation where you are giving more than you have to give. Over time, this can lead to feelings of burnout, resentment, and frustration.

Boundaries are vital because they allow you to:

- **Protect your emotional energy**: Ensuring you have the space and time to recharge.
- **Honor your needs**: Affirming that your well-being is a priority, not an afterthought.
- **Cultivate mutual respect in relationships**: Clear boundaries help others understand your limits and foster respect and healthy interaction.
- **Stay connected to your true self**: When your boundaries are clear, you are less likely to compromise on your values or sacrifice your well-being for others.

Boundaries serve as a way to safeguard your emotional core, ensuring that you can show up as your best self in your relationships, work, and personal life without feeling drained or compromised.

The Link Between Boundaries and Self-Compassion

Setting boundaries is a powerful form of self-compassion. It's recognizing that you deserve the same care and respect that you offer to others. Often, we think that saying "yes" to everything makes us kinder or more generous, but in reality, it can lead to overextension, stress, and even resentment.

True generosity and kindness start with being kind to yourself—by giving yourself the space to recharge, by protecting your emotional energy, and by allowing yourself to say "no" when you need to.

When you set boundaries, you're acknowledging that your well-being matters just as much as the well-being of those around you. This isn't selfish—it's necessary. You can't pour from an empty cup, and if you're constantly giving to others without creating space for yourself, you'll eventually run dry.

Self-compassion means allowing yourself to set limits, to say "no" without guilt, and to create healthy distances in situations that drain your energy.

By doing so, you're practicing emotional self-care, ensuring that you have the inner resources to handle life's challenges and maintain balance.

Common Fears About Setting Boundaries

For many people, the idea of setting boundaries brings up discomfort or fear. You might worry that setting a boundary will upset others, create conflict, or make you seem selfish. You might even fear that by enforcing boundaries, you'll disappoint people or damage relationships.

But here's the truth: Setting healthy boundaries does not make you selfish—it makes you emotionally healthy. Boundaries ensure that your relationships are balanced, respectful, and mutually supportive.

And people who genuinely care about you will respect your boundaries because they understand that you need them to feel secure and well.

Here are some common fears that may arise when thinking about setting boundaries:

- **Fear of conflict**: You might worry that saying "no" will create tension or conflict with others. But remember, boundary-setting is not about creating conflict—it's about creating clarity. In most cases, people appreciate knowing your limits because it sets clear expectations for both sides.
- **Fear of being seen as selfish**: There's often a fear that by setting boundaries, you're being selfish or self-centered. But boundaries are not about shutting people out—they're about protecting your emotional energy so that you can show up fully for yourself and others.
- **Fear of rejection**: You might worry that setting a boundary will push people away or make them think less of you. However, healthy boundaries are the foundation of healthy relationships. They help build trust and respect, rather than eroding them.

In reality, setting boundaries creates stronger, more authentic relationships because they are built on mutual respect and understanding.

When you respect your own needs, others are more likely to respect them, too.

The Types of Boundaries You Need

Boundaries come in many forms and can vary depending on

your needs and life circumstances. Here are a few key types of boundaries that can help you protect your emotional energy and stay connected to your true self:

- **Emotional Boundaries**: These involve protecting your emotional well-being by deciding what kinds of emotional interactions you engage in. For example, you may set a boundary around how much emotional labor you take on in relationships, or how you respond to toxic or negative conversations.
- **Time Boundaries**: Time boundaries are about protecting your schedule and ensuring that you have the time and space you need for rest, personal projects, or self-care. They might involve saying no to commitments when you're already stretched too thin, or setting limits on how much time you dedicate to certain activities or people.
- **Mental Boundaries**: Mental boundaries protect your mental energy and focus. This might mean setting limits on how much you allow yourself to engage with stress-inducing conversations or avoiding discussions that drain your mental resources.
- **Work Boundaries**: At work, boundaries ensure that you maintain a healthy balance between your professional responsibilities and your personal life. This could include setting limits on how available you are outside of work hours or clarifying expectations around your workload.
- **Physical Boundaries**: These refer to the space and touch you are comfortable with, ensuring that your physical well-being is respected in your relationships and interactions with others.

Boundaries are not about shutting others out—they're about creating the space you need to thrive. By setting boundaries, you create a framework for healthier, more respectful interactions in all areas of your life.

Exercise: Identify Three Situations Where You Need Stronger Boundaries

Now that you understand the importance of boundaries, it's time to reflect on your own life and identify where you might need stronger boundaries.

This exercise will guide you through the process of recognizing areas where your boundaries need to be reinforced and help you plan specific actions to maintain them.

Step 1: Reflect on Areas of Your Life Needing Stronger Boundaries

Start by thinking about the different areas of your life: work, relationships, personal commitments, and even how you spend your free time.

Consider where you feel drained, overwhelmed, or like your needs are being overlooked. These are often the areas where stronger boundaries are needed.

Here are some prompts to help guide your reflection:

- **Where do I feel emotionally drained or overextended?**
  Is there a relationship or situation in your life where you feel constantly drained or overwhelmed? This could be a friendship that has become too demanding, a work environment that spills over into your personal life, or social commitments that leave you feeling depleted.
- **When do I feel like I'm putting others' needs above my own?**
  Consider times when you've said "yes" when you really wanted to say "no." Are you sacrificing your own needs in order to avoid disappointing others or to maintain peace?
- **Where do I feel resentment building?**
  Resentment is often a signal that boundaries have been

crossed. Reflect on situations or people that leave you feeling resentful, as this is often a sign that you need to set clearer limits.

Step 2: Identify Three Specific Situations Needing Stronger Boundaries

Once you've reflected on where your boundaries are being tested, identify three specific situations where you need stronger boundaries. Be as clear and specific as possible.

For example:

- **At work**: "I need to set a boundary around checking emails outside of work hours."
- **In relationships**: "I need to set a boundary around how much time I spend helping a friend who constantly asks for favors without giving back."
- **Personal life**: "I need to set a boundary around making time for myself, even when there are competing demands from others."

Step 3: Plan Specific Actions to Enforce These Boundaries

Now that you've identified the areas where you need stronger boundaries, plan specific actions to enforce them. Boundaries are only effective when they're clearly communicated and consistently maintained.

For each situation, consider:

- **What boundary do I need to set?**
  Be specific about what needs to change. For example, "I need to stop taking work calls after 6 p.m." or "I need to decline social invitations when I'm feeling burned out."
- **How will I communicate this boundary?**
  Think about how you'll clearly and kindly communicate your boundary. For example, "I'm really focused on maintaining a better work-life balance, so I won't be available after 6 p.m." or "I've been feeling overwhelmed

lately, and I need to take some time for myself, so I won't be able to help with that right now."

- **How will I reinforce the boundary if it's challenged?**
Consider how you'll respond if someone crosses your boundary or pressures you to compromise. Plan to restate your boundary calmly and firmly: "I understand this is important, but I need to respect the limits I've set for myself."

Reflection on the Exercise

How did it feel to identify areas in your life where stronger boundaries are needed? Did any particular situations stand out as places where you've been overextending yourself? How confident do you feel about enforcing those boundaries moving forward?

Setting boundaries is an act of self-respect and self-care. It may feel uncomfortable at first, especially if you're used to prioritizing others' needs over your own.

But with time, you'll find that boundaries protect not only your emotional energy but also your sense of self-worth and well-being.

Takeaway

Today, you took a crucial step toward protecting your emotional energy by identifying areas where stronger boundaries are needed in your life.

By setting clear, healthy boundaries, you are honoring your needs and ensuring that your relationships remain balanced, respectful, and mutually supportive.

As you continue on this journey, remember that setting boundaries is an ongoing practice. It's not about pushing others away—it's about creating the space you need to thrive emotionally, mentally, and physically.

And the more you practice, the more confident and empowered you'll feel in protecting your own well-being.

Tomorrow, we'll continue exploring resilience by learning how to embrace discomfort and transform it into emotional growth.

But for today, take a moment to appreciate the boundaries you've set and the emotional freedom you're creating for yourself.

Remember: *Healthy boundaries are a form of self-respect. They protect your energy, honor your needs, and allow you to show up fully for yourself and others.*

DAY 10: RELEASING EMOTIONAL BAGGAGE

Welcome to Day 10. Over the past few days, you've done significant inner work—setting healthy boundaries, practicing self-compassion, and expanding your emotional vocabulary.

Today, we're diving into something that often remains hidden yet weighs heavily on our ability to live freely and authentically: *emotional baggage.*

Carrying emotional baggage is like walking through life with a heavy backpack you didn't even realize you were wearing. It might be filled with old regrets, unprocessed pain, or unresolved feelings that you've been carrying for years.

While you've learned to manage the weight, it's there, quietly shaping how you see the world, interact with others, and view yourself.

The emotional weight of the past limits your ability to connect fully with your authentic self and move forward with clarity and peace.

Today is about releasing that weight. It's about identifying what no longer serves you, acknowledging its impact, and consciously choosing to let it go. This isn't about denying the past or pretending difficult things didn't happen—it's about deciding not to let those experiences define or control your present and future.

By releasing emotional baggage, you're making space for healing, lightness, and a deeper connection to yourself.

What Is Emotional Baggage?

Emotional baggage consists of the unresolved emotions, unhealed wounds, and limiting beliefs that we accumulate from past experiences. It might come from difficult relationships, past mistakes, or events that left you feeling hurt, betrayed, or disempowered.

While these experiences shaped who you are, continuing to carry the emotional weight of them can prevent you from growing into who you are meant to become.

This emotional baggage can show up in many ways:

- **Unresolved Guilt**: You may carry guilt from mistakes or decisions that didn't turn out as planned. This lingering guilt can manifest as self-criticism or self-doubt, keeping you stuck in a loop of regret.
- **Resentment**: Holding onto anger or resentment toward someone who wronged you can feel justified, but it ultimately keeps you tied to that person or situation, draining your emotional energy.
- **Limiting Beliefs**: These are the stories you've internalized about yourself based on past experiences, like "I'm not good enough," "I always fail," or "I can't trust people." These beliefs act as invisible barriers that hold you back from embracing new opportunities and relationships.

Carrying these emotions without resolution creates emotional clutter, clouding your ability to experience the present moment fully. It's like driving through life with a rearview mirror that's constantly showing you the past, making it difficult to see where you're going.

But releasing emotional baggage allows you to reclaim your emotional space, lighten your load, and move forward with more clarity and peace.

Why Releasing Emotional Baggage Matters

Releasing emotional baggage is a key step in reconnecting with your true self and living more authentically. When you hold onto past pain, unresolved emotions, or limiting beliefs, you're tethered to the past in ways that impact your present.

These emotional weights can affect your self-esteem, your relationships, and your overall sense of joy and fulfillment.

Letting go of emotional baggage helps you:

- **Reconnect with your authentic self**: When you release old wounds or limiting beliefs, you free yourself to live more fully in alignment with who you are today, rather than being defined by past experiences.
- **Create space for healing**: By letting go of emotional baggage, you open yourself up to healing. You allow yourself to process emotions that have been buried and to move through them with compassion.
- **Foster emotional resilience**: The process of releasing emotional baggage strengthens your emotional resilience. You learn that you are capable of moving through difficult emotions without letting them control you.

Releasing what no longer serves you is about choosing freedom. It's about deciding that the past, while important, will not dictate your future.

It's an act of self-love and self-respect, allowing you to step into the next chapter of your life with more openness, lightness, and clarity.

The Emotional Weight You've Been Carrying

We all carry some form of emotional baggage, and often, we don't even realize it until we start paying attention. It might be the guilt you feel every time you think about a decision you wish you'd made differently. Or maybe it's the fear that surfaces in relationships because of past betrayals.

Whatever the form, emotional baggage tends to linger in the background, subtly influencing how we navigate life and relationships.

For example:

- **You may avoid taking risks** because you still carry the fear of failure from a past experience where things didn't go as planned.
- **You may struggle to trust others** because you're holding onto the pain of past betrayals.
- **You may find it hard to forgive yourself** for mistakes, carrying guilt or shame that clouds your self-worth.

Emotional baggage can also show up in your body—tightness in your chest, tension in your shoulders, or that sinking feeling in your stomach when old memories resurface.

These are signs that unresolved emotions are weighing you down, even if you've learned to live with them.

But today, you're giving yourself permission to release that weight. By recognizing the emotional baggage you've been carrying, you take the first step toward healing. It's time to let go of the past and make space for the present.

The Power of Letting Go

Letting go is not about forgetting or minimizing your

experiences.

It's about acknowledging the impact those experiences have had on you, learning from them, and then choosing not to carry the emotional weight any longer. It's about freeing yourself from the narrative that you have to be defined by your past.

Here's what letting go can do for you:

- **It frees up emotional energy**: When you release old pain, you create space for new, healthier emotions to take root. You can focus on joy, growth, and connection, rather than being stuck in old patterns of hurt.
- **It empowers you to redefine yourself**: You are not your past. By letting go, you reclaim your power to define who you are today and who you want to be moving forward.
- **It brings closure and healing**: Letting go isn't about erasing the past, but about healing from it. When you release the emotional charge associated with past experiences, you can look at them from a place of peace rather than pain.

Letting go takes courage. It requires you to face emotions you may have buried for a long time. But the reward is emotional freedom and a deeper connection with your true self.

Exercise: Write Down Three Past Experiences You're Ready to Release

Today's exercise will guide you through the process of identifying and releasing emotional baggage.

This is a personal and reflective practice that will help you let go of the past and create space for healing.

Step 1: Identify Three Past Experiences You're Ready to Release

Take a moment to reflect on the emotional baggage you've been carrying. Think about three specific experiences, memories, or unresolved feelings that you're ready to release. These could be:

- A past relationship that ended painfully, where you still carry feelings of regret or resentment.
- A mistake or decision that you've been holding onto with guilt or shame.
- A limiting belief that was formed from a difficult experience, such as "I'm not worthy" or "I'll never be enough."

These are the experiences that resurface in your mind and weigh on your heart. By identifying them, you're acknowledging their presence and taking the first step toward releasing them.

Step 2: Create a Ritual for Letting Them Go

Rituals provide a symbolic and emotional way to mark the process of letting go. Creating a simple ritual can help you bring closure to these experiences and release their emotional hold on you.

Here are a few ideas for your ritual:

- **Write a Letter**: Write a letter to the past experiences, feelings, or people you're letting go of. In the letter, express everything you need to say. Allow yourself to acknowledge the pain, the lessons learned, and the emotions tied to these experiences. Once you've written the letter, you can choose to keep it as a symbol of release or burn it (safely) as a symbolic way of letting go.
- **Visualization**: Sit in a quiet space and close your eyes. Visualize the emotional baggage you're carrying as a heavy weight. Imagine yourself taking off that weight—whether it's a backpack, a ball and chain, or something else—and watch it dissolve, float away, or be absorbed into the earth. As you breathe deeply, feel yourself becoming lighter with each breath.
- **Release through Nature**: If you're near a body of water

or nature, you can use the elements to symbolize release. Write down the experiences you're letting go of on small pieces of paper, and release them into a flowing stream, river, or fire (safely). Let the current or the flames carry away the emotional weight.

Step 3: Reflect on the Process

After completing your ritual, take some time to reflect on how it felt to release these past experiences. Did you feel a sense of lightness or relief? Was there any resistance?

Remember that letting go is a process—it's okay if some emotions take time to release fully.

Reflection on the Exercise

How did it feel to identify the emotional baggage you've been carrying? Did certain experiences stand out as particularly heavy? How did it feel to create a ritual for letting them go?

Releasing emotional baggage is a journey, not a one-time event. As you continue this process, you'll find more space for emotional clarity, healing, and self-connection.

Takeaway

Today, you took a courageous step toward emotional freedom by identifying and releasing emotional baggage. By letting go of past experiences that no longer serve you, you've made room for healing, growth, and a deeper connection to your authentic self.

As you move forward, remember that releasing emotional baggage is an ongoing practice. Each time you choose to let go of something that weighs you down, you create more space for joy, self-acceptance, and possibility.

Tomorrow, we'll continue our journey by exploring how to build emotional flexibility and resilience.

But for today, take a moment to honor the emotional lightness and clarity you've created for yourself.

Remember: *Releasing emotional baggage isn't about forgetting the past—it's about freeing yourself from its hold so you can fully embrace the present and the future.*

DAY 11: THE DISCIPLINE OF SELF-CARE

Welcome to Day 11. After the significant work you've done in releasing emotional baggage, today is about filling that newly created space with something just as vital: *self-care*.

While it may seem like a buzzword in today's wellness culture, true self-care is far more profound than the occasional spa day or time off. It is a *discipline*, an intentional, structured practice of caring for your mind, body, and spirit daily. It's about making yourself a priority—not in a self-indulgent way, but as an act of self-love.

For the Holistic Personal Development Enthusiast, like you, self-care goes beyond surface-level pampering. It's a way of creating emotional balance, building resilience, and ensuring that you are strong enough to face the demands of life while still nurturing your own well-being.

And yet, despite knowing its importance, many people struggle with guilt when it comes to prioritizing self-care.

Today, we're going to explore how to make self-care a guilt-free, non-negotiable part of your life and why it's necessary to ensure that your emotional and physical energy are sustained in a balanced, healthy way.

What Does Self-Care Really Mean?

Self-care is often reduced to activities like treating yourself to a nice meal or having a relaxing evening.

While those are certainly forms of self-care, *true self-care* runs deeper. It's about creating practices that nurture your mental, emotional, and physical well-being consistently—so that you can show up fully in your life, relationships, and work.

Here's what self-care involves:

- **Mental Self-Care**: Protecting your mental health by creating boundaries around stressful tasks, allowing yourself time to reflect, unwind, and mentally recharge.
- **Emotional Self-Care**: Practicing self-compassion, acknowledging your feelings without judgment, and creating space to process difficult emotions in a healthy way.
- **Physical Self-Care**: Taking care of your body through regular movement, proper nutrition, restful sleep, and listening to your body's needs.
- **Spiritual Self-Care**: Whether through meditation, journaling, or mindfulness, connecting with your inner self and reflecting on the deeper aspects of your life.

Self-care is not about escaping from your life but about sustaining your ability to live it fully. It's about making sure that you have the resources to face life's challenges with strength, calm, and resilience, and that you are consistently refilling your well of emotional, mental, and physical energy.

The Importance of Making Self-Care a Discipline

Self-care is not something you do only when you have time—it's something you *make time for*. It's a discipline that becomes a regular part of your daily routine, no different from brushing your teeth or eating a meal. When self-care is treated as a luxury, it's easy to neglect it during busy or stressful times, which is when you need it the most.

By integrating self-care into your daily routine, you're ensuring that you're consistently refueling your body, mind, and spirit, preventing burnout before it happens.

Here's why self-care as a discipline matters:

- **Prevents burnout**: When you practice self-care regularly, you're less likely to reach a point of emotional or physical exhaustion. Instead of waiting until you're completely depleted to recharge, you're consistently topping up your energy levels.
- **Reinforces self-worth**: By prioritizing self-care, you're reinforcing the belief that your well-being is important. It affirms your worth by reminding yourself that you deserve care, attention, and time for yourself.
- **Supports emotional resilience**: Regular self-care builds a buffer against stress. It allows you to remain grounded and calm even when life throws challenges your way because you've made a habit of taking care of your emotional health.
- **Nurtures long-term balance**: When self-care is part of your daily routine, you're creating sustainable habits that keep you in balance—physically, emotionally, and mentally—over the long term.

The discipline of self-care is not about perfection. It's about creating small, intentional habits that protect your well-being on a daily basis. Think of it as an investment in your future self—ensuring that you have the strength and clarity to handle whatever life brings.

Releasing the Guilt Around Self-Care

One of the greatest barriers to self-care is guilt. Many people, especially those in caring roles or high-demand professions, feel guilty for taking time for themselves. They worry that prioritizing their own well-being is selfish or that they should be using that time to help others or be more productive.

But here's the truth: *self-care is not selfish*. It's essential.

When you take care of yourself, you're not only protecting your own well-being—you're also ensuring that you have the energy, focus, and emotional strength to show up for the people and tasks that matter in your life.

Without self-care, you can't pour into others from a full cup. You'll be running on empty, and eventually, that will catch up with you.

Releasing guilt starts with reframing how you think about self-care. Instead of seeing it as a luxury or something you do when everything else is finished, recognize that self-care is what makes everything else possible.

It's the foundation for all other aspects of your life. When you practice self-care, you're giving yourself the resources you need to show up as your best, most present self.

Integrating Self-Care Into Your Busy Life

One of the challenges people face when it comes to self-care is time. Between work, family, and personal responsibilities, it can feel like there's no room left for yourself.

But the good news is that self-care doesn't have to be time-consuming or complicated. It's not about carving out hours each day for elaborate rituals—it's about finding small, simple ways to nurture yourself regularly.

Here are some ways to integrate self-care into your busy life:

- **Start small**: Self-care doesn't have to be grand. Even five minutes of mindful breathing, stretching, or journaling can make a big difference in how you feel. The key is consistency—making self-care a regular part of your day, even in small doses.
- **Schedule it like a non-negotiable**: Treat self-care like any other important commitment. Block out time on your calendar for it, whether it's a 10-minute walk, an evening bath, or 15 minutes of meditation. When you treat it as a non-negotiable, you're more likely to follow through.
- **Make it part of your routine**: The easiest way to ensure self-care happens is to build it into your daily routine. Pair it with something you already do, like journaling with your morning coffee or stretching before bed.
- **Release the "all-or-nothing" mindset**: You don't need an hour of free time to practice self-care. Even a few minutes can have a positive impact. Let go of the idea that it's only worth it if it's a big, time-consuming act. Self-care is about quality, not quantity.

When self-care becomes part of your daily routine, you'll start to feel the benefits in every area of your life. You'll feel more grounded, more focused, and more connected to yourself.

And over time, these small acts of care will add up, creating a foundation of resilience, balance, and well-being.

Exercise: Identify One Self-Care Practice You Can Do Daily

Now that you understand the importance of self-care, it's time to put it into action. This exercise will help you identify one self-care practice that you can commit to doing daily for the next week.

Step 1: Reflect on What You Need Most Right Now

Before choosing a self-care practice, take a moment to reflect on what you need most in this moment. Are you feeling emotionally drained, physically exhausted, or mentally overwhelmed?

Understanding where you feel depleted will help you choose a self-care practice that meets your current needs.

Here are some prompts to help guide your reflection:

- **What part of me feels the most depleted—emotionally, physically, or mentally?**
- **What activities make me feel recharged, grounded, or more at ease?**
- **Where do I need to create space for myself in my daily routine?**

Step 2: Choose One Self-Care Practice

Based on your reflection, choose one self-care practice that aligns with what you need most. This could be something simple and manageable, like:

- **A 10-minute morning meditation** to center yourself before the day begins.
- **A daily walk outside** to clear your mind and connect with nature.
- **Journaling for five minutes** at the end of the day to reflect and process your emotions.
- **Stretching or gentle yoga** to release physical tension and relax your body.
- **Reading for pleasure** for 10 minutes before bed to unwind and nurture your mind.

Choose something that feels sustainable and nourishing—something you

DAY 12: BUILDING SELF-TRUST

Welcome to Day 12. So far, you've worked on letting go of emotional baggage, practicing self-care, and creating a deeper connection with your authentic self.

Today, we'll focus on something fundamental to all of these practices: *self-trust*.

Self-trust is the cornerstone of confidence and resilience. It's about having faith in your own ability to make decisions, navigate challenges, and guide yourself toward what's best for you.

Trusting yourself means you believe in your intuition and your inner wisdom, even when external circumstances—or the opinions of others—might cast doubt.

But self-trust isn't always easy. You might have internalized doubt from past experiences or external expectations that caused you to second-guess yourself. Maybe you've relied on others' advice or sought external validation, leaving you disconnected from your own inner compass.

Today, we'll focus on rebuilding that connection, learning to trust your decisions and your ability to navigate life with confidence and clarity.

Trusting yourself isn't about always being right; it's about trusting that you will be okay, even if the path is uncertain or if things don't go exactly as planned. You are resilient. You have what it takes to adapt, learn, and grow.

And it starts with listening to that inner voice that always knows what's right for *you*.

Why Self-Trust Matters

Self-trust is the foundation of a balanced, empowered life. When you trust yourself, you're not constantly seeking reassurance or approval from others. Instead, you feel grounded in your own decisions, confident that you're capable of handling whatever comes your way.

Without self-trust, it's easy to feel lost or disconnected from your true self, relying too heavily on external guidance or fearing that you'll make the "wrong" choice.

Here's why self-trust is essential to your growth:

- **It fosters confidence**: Trusting yourself naturally leads to greater confidence in your abilities, choices, and direction in life. You no longer need to second-guess yourself at every turn.
- **It builds resilience**: Self-trust helps you remain steady, even in uncertainty. You trust that you have the tools to navigate challenges, adapt to unexpected outcomes, and grow from them.
- **It strengthens your intuition**: The more you trust yourself, the more you strengthen your connection to your intuition—that inner voice that knows what feels right for you, even when logic or external factors don't fully explain it.
- **It leads to authentic decisions**: When you trust yourself, your decisions come from a place of alignment with your values, desires, and authentic self. You're less likely to be swayed by fear or outside opinions.

Self-trust isn't about perfection. It's not about making flawless decisions every time. It's about believing that you have the capacity to navigate both success and failure with grace and growth. It's knowing that, regardless of the outcome, you can handle it—and that you're worthy of trusting yourself through every step of your journey.

The Power of Intuition in Self-Trust

One of the key aspects of self-trust is learning to listen to—and act on—your intuition.

Your intuition is your inner compass, a guiding voice that often knows the answer before your conscious mind has fully processed it. It's that deep, internal sense that tells you when something feels right or wrong, even if you can't always explain why.

For many, trusting intuition can feel challenging, especially in a world that prioritizes logic, data, and external validation. You might worry that your intuition will lead you astray, or that it's not "reliable" enough to trust.

But intuition is based on a lifetime of experience, learning, and subconscious wisdom. When you listen to your intuition, you're tapping into a reservoir of knowledge that extends beyond mere facts.

Trusting your intuition is a powerful way to build self-trust. It's the act of believing in your own inner knowing and following what feels right for *you*, even if it doesn't always make sense to others.

Over time, as you strengthen your relationship with your intuition, you'll find that it becomes easier to make decisions that align with your true self.

Here are ways intuition shows up in your life:

- **A gut feeling**: This is the most common form of intuition. It's that feeling in your body—whether it's a sense of ease or discomfort—that signals whether a choice is right or

wrong.
- **Clarity without logic**: Sometimes, you just *know* something without having all the logical reasons to back it up. This is intuition guiding you.
- **A pull toward a decision**: Intuition can feel like being drawn in a certain direction, even if it's unexpected or goes against the grain of what's rational.

Learning to trust your intuition is key to building self-trust because it reinforces the idea that *you know what's best for you*—even if it doesn't always follow conventional wisdom.

Overcoming Self-Doubt to Build Self-Trust

Self-doubt is often the biggest obstacle to building self-trust. Past mistakes, criticism, or fear of failure can make you second-guess yourself, leading you to seek validation from others rather than trusting your own judgment. But self-doubt is part of the human experience. It's natural to feel unsure at times, but allowing it to control your decisions can leave you feeling disconnected from your own inner power.

Here's how you can overcome self-doubt and cultivate greater self-trust:

- **Start with small decisions**: If trusting yourself feels overwhelming, start with small, everyday decisions. Whether it's choosing what to eat, what task to prioritize, or how to spend your free time, practice trusting your own judgment in these moments. Over time, these small choices will build your confidence.
- **Reflect on your past successes**: Think back to times when you trusted yourself and things worked out well. What decisions did you make based on your intuition or inner wisdom? Reflecting on these moments can remind you that you *can* trust yourself.

- **Acknowledge the fear but move forward**: Self-trust doesn't mean the absence of fear. It means acknowledging the fear and making the decision anyway, knowing that even if things don't go perfectly, you'll learn and grow from the experience.
- **Give yourself permission to make mistakes**: No one makes the right decision 100% of the time. Building self-trust is about believing in your ability to handle the outcomes, whether they're what you expected or not. Mistakes are not a reflection of your worth—they're opportunities to grow.

Each time you trust yourself, even in small ways, you're strengthening that inner muscle of confidence. Over time, trusting your own judgment will become more natural, and you'll feel more grounded and capable in making decisions that align with your authentic self.

Exercise: Reflect on a Recent Decision You Made Based on Intuition

Today's exercise is designed to help you connect more deeply with your intuition and build self-trust by reflecting on a recent decision you made based on your inner knowing.

This practice will give you the space to explore how it felt to trust yourself in that moment and how your intuition guided you.

Step 1: Recall a Recent Decision Made from Intuition

Think about a recent decision you made where you relied on your intuition, rather than overthinking or seeking outside advice. It could be a small decision, like reaching out to someone unexpectedly, or a larger one, like making a career shift or setting a personal boundary.

Here are some prompts to guide your reflection:

- What was the decision, and what prompted it?
- How did you know it was the right choice for you?
- Did you feel any internal resistance or doubt before making the decision?

Step 2: Reflect on How It Felt to Trust Yourself

Now that you've identified the decision, take some time to reflect on how it felt to trust your intuition in that moment. Did you feel a sense of relief or clarity? Or was there some fear or discomfort that you had to work through?

The goal is to explore your emotional and physical responses to trusting yourself.

Here are some additional questions to consider:

- **How did trusting your intuition feel in your body?**
  Did you notice a sense of lightness, calm, or tension when you made the decision?
- **What emotions surfaced as you followed your intuition?**
  Did you feel empowered, anxious, or uncertain? Reflect on the mix of emotions that came up.
- **How did you feel afterward?**
  After the decision was made, did you feel more confident or at peace? Or did doubts creep in? Reflect on whether following your intuition felt validating, even if the outcome wasn't clear at the time.

Step 3: Affirm Your Self-Trust

Finally, take a moment to affirm your self-trust. Regardless of the outcome of the decision, honor the fact that you trusted your intuition and inner wisdom. Write down a few affirmations that reinforce your self-trust, such as:

- *"I trust my intuition to guide me."*
- *"I can handle whatever comes from trusting my decisions."*
- *"I have the wisdom and strength to navigate life's*

uncertainties."

By affirming your ability to trust yourself, you're reinforcing the belief that you are capable, resilient, and wise.

Reflection on the Exercise

How did it feel to reflect on a decision you made based on intuition? Did you notice any patterns in how your body or emotions responded? Were there moments of doubt or clarity?

Reflecting on these moments helps strengthen your self-trust, reminding you that you *can* trust your inner guidance, even when the path ahead feels uncertain.

Takeaway

Today, you took an important step toward building self-trust by reflecting on a recent decision guided by your intuition. Each time you trust yourself—whether in small or significant ways—you strengthen your confidence and connection to your true self. Trusting your intuition doesn't mean always being right; it means believing that you have the inner resources to navigate whatever comes your way.

As you move forward, continue to practice self-trust in both everyday choices and larger decisions. Remember, self-trust is built one decision at a time, and with each choice, you grow stronger in your ability to guide yourself through life.

Tomorrow, we'll dive deeper into cultivating resilience and emotional strength. But for today, take a moment to celebrate the trust you've cultivated in yourself.

Remember: *Trusting yourself is an act of courage and self-love. It's about believing in your ability to navigate life's challenges with confidence, resilience, and inner wisdom.*

DAY 13: MANAGING EMOTIONAL TRIGGERS

Welcome to Day 13. Throughout this journey, you've explored the depths of self-care, self-trust, and emotional resilience. Today's focus is crucial in continuing to build that emotional strength: *managing emotional triggers*.

We all have emotional triggers—those moments when an external event causes an intense internal reaction. It could be a word someone says, a gesture, or a situation that makes you feel like you've suddenly lost control of your emotions.

But while triggers are natural, they don't have to dictate how you respond.

The key is learning to recognize, understand, and manage these triggers so they don't control you.

Today, you'll gain a deeper understanding of what triggers you, why they affect you so deeply, and how you can create space between the trigger and your reaction.

This practice will help you build emotional resilience and stay more grounded, no matter what life throws your way.

What Are Emotional Triggers?

An emotional trigger is anything—an event, a comment, or even a memory—that causes a strong emotional reaction in you.

Triggers often hit deep-rooted vulnerabilities, stirring emotions that might feel out of proportion to the situation at hand. These reactions happen fast, almost automatically, as though you're suddenly transported back to an unresolved emotional experience.

For example:

- **Being interrupted in a meeting** might trigger feelings of frustration or inadequacy, especially if you've struggled to have your voice heard in the past.
- **A friend canceling plans at the last minute** might stir feelings of rejection or abandonment, particularly if you've experienced similar letdowns before.
- **Receiving constructive feedback** might feel like harsh criticism if you've been judged or overly criticized in previous environments.

Triggers are deeply personal, shaped by our past experiences, traumas, and unprocessed emotions.

But the more aware you are of them, the better you can manage your reactions and prevent those triggers from controlling your emotional state.

Why Managing Triggers Is Important

Emotional triggers can disrupt your sense of calm and make you react in ways that don't reflect your true self. Left unmanaged, triggers can strain relationships, lead to stress or anxiety, and even erode your self-confidence.

But when you manage your triggers, you create space between the trigger and your reaction. You give yourself time to pause, reflect, and respond with greater emotional balance and intention.

Here's why learning to manage your emotional triggers is

essential:

- **It builds emotional resilience**: Triggers are inevitable, but how you respond to them determines your emotional resilience. By managing your reactions, you'll find it easier to navigate difficult situations without being overwhelmed.
- **It empowers you to choose your responses**: Instead of reacting impulsively when you're triggered, managing your triggers allows you to choose your response. This leads to better outcomes in relationships, work, and life.
- **It protects your emotional energy**: Emotional triggers can drain you if left unchecked. When you manage them, you conserve your emotional energy and can stay focused on what truly matters.
- **It deepens your self-awareness**: Every trigger is a doorway to deeper self-understanding. Recognizing your triggers allows you to explore unresolved emotions or past wounds, giving you the opportunity to heal.

Managing triggers isn't about denying your feelings. It's about acknowledging them, understanding their roots, and choosing how to respond—rather than letting the trigger control you.

How Emotional Triggers Work

When you're triggered, your brain interprets the situation as a threat—whether real or perceived. This activates the amygdala, the part of your brain responsible for processing emotions, and triggers the fight, flight, or freeze response.

This response is designed to protect you from danger, but in the context of emotional triggers, it can make you overreact to situations that aren't truly threatening.

For instance:

- **If you've been criticized harshly in the past**, constructive feedback might feel like an attack, triggering feelings of

shame or anger.
- **If you've experienced rejection in relationships**, a small slight from a friend could evoke strong feelings of abandonment or unworthiness.
- **If you've faced instability**, sudden changes or uncertainty can provoke intense anxiety as your brain tries to protect you from the perceived threat of chaos or loss of control.

Your emotional response to these triggers is shaped by past experiences. The intensity of your reaction often comes not from the current situation but from the emotional weight it carries from unresolved issues.

Understanding this helps you approach your triggers with more compassion and less judgment.

Steps to Managing Emotional Triggers

Managing emotional triggers involves breaking the automatic cycle of reaction by becoming more mindful of your emotions.

The goal is to create a pause between the trigger and your response, allowing you to choose how you want to react rather than being overwhelmed by emotions.

Here's how you can manage your emotional triggers:

1. **Recognize the trigger**: The first step in managing emotional triggers is recognizing when you're being triggered. Pay attention to physical sensations (such as a racing heart or tightness in the chest) and emotional cues (like sudden anger or anxiety). These are signs that you've been triggered.
2. **Acknowledge the emotion**: When you're triggered, don't suppress or ignore the emotion. Acknowledge what you're feeling without judgment. Label the emotion—whether it's anger, fear, sadness, or

frustration—and remind yourself that it's okay to feel triggered. This step helps create distance between you and the emotional reaction.

3. **Pause before reacting**: Instead of reacting impulsively, give yourself permission to pause. Take a few deep breaths or step away from the situation if possible. The pause is crucial because it allows your rational brain (the prefrontal cortex) to engage, giving you time to respond thoughtfully.

4. **Examine the root cause**: Triggers are often tied to unresolved emotions from the past. Ask yourself, "What's this really about?" Is this reaction based on the present situation, or is it bringing up old wounds or fears? Understanding the deeper cause can help you approach the situation with more clarity and compassion.

5. **Choose your response**: After you've paused and reflected, consciously choose how to respond. This might mean addressing the situation calmly, setting a boundary, or simply deciding not to engage. The key is responding in a way that aligns with your values and long-term emotional well-being.

Exercise: Create a Trigger Map

Today's exercise is designed to help you identify and map your emotional triggers. By creating a "trigger map," you'll gain clarity on the situations that cause strong emotional reactions and develop strategies to manage them effectively.

Step 1: Identify Your Triggers

Start by reflecting on recent situations where you experienced an intense emotional reaction. Write down the event, what emotion surfaced, and any patterns you notice. These might be moments of frustration, anger, fear, or sadness.

Try to be specific about what triggered the emotion.

Here are some prompts to help guide your reflection:
- **What situations tend to trigger strong emotional reactions in me?**
- **What emotions surface when I'm triggered?**
- **Are there specific people, places, or situations that consistently trigger me?**

Example:
- **Trigger**: A colleague dismissing my idea in a meeting.
  Emotion: Frustration, hurt.
  Root cause: Fear of being undervalued or dismissed, which stems from past experiences where my voice wasn't heard.

Step 2: Map Your Triggers

Now that you've identified your triggers, create a visual map that links the triggers to the emotions they bring up.

This can help you spot patterns and gain insight into why certain situations affect you so strongly. In your map, include:

- The trigger (the situation or event)
- The immediate emotional response
- The deeper root cause (any past experiences or insecurities that may be contributing)

Example:
- **Trigger**: Being ignored during a discussion.
  Emotion: Anger, frustration.
  Root cause: Past experiences of being dismissed, leading to feelings of inadequacy.

Step 3: Develop Strategies for Managing Triggers

Once you've mapped your triggers, develop strategies for managing them when they arise. These strategies should focus on creating a pause, processing the emotion, and choosing how to respond.

Here are some strategies to consider:

- **Breathing techniques**: When triggered, take a few deep breaths to calm your nervous system and create space before reacting.
- **Positive affirmations**: Remind yourself, "I am safe. I am in control of how I respond." This can help ground you in the present moment.
- **Physical grounding**: Focus on your physical surroundings to bring your mind back to the present. Notice the feel of your chair, the temperature in the room, or the sounds around you.
- **Journaling**: If you're feeling overwhelmed, step away and write down what you're experiencing. This can help you process the emotion without acting on it impulsively.

Example:

- **Strategy**: When I feel ignored or dismissed, I will pause and take five deep breaths. I'll remind myself that my worth is not dependent on others' reactions. If needed, I'll journal about my feelings later to gain clarity and process the emotion fully.

Reflection on the Exercise

How did it feel to map your emotional triggers? Did you notice any patterns in your reactions or deeper root causes? This exercise is about increasing your self-awareness and gaining clarity on why certain situations affect you so deeply.

By identifying your triggers, you've taken the first step toward managing them with greater intention and emotional balance.

Takeaway

Today, you've made significant progress in understanding and managing your emotional triggers by creating a trigger map and developing strategies to handle them.

Managing triggers is a lifelong practice of self-awareness, self-compassion, and mindful response. With this awareness, you're better equipped to navigate emotionally charged situations with grace and intention, rather than being swept away by reactivity.

As you continue this journey, remember that managing triggers is not about avoiding difficult emotions but about responding to them with understanding and calm.

Each time you choose to pause and reflect, you strengthen your emotional resilience and reclaim control over your responses.

Tomorrow, we'll dive deeper into cultivating emotional resilience and handling stress in a balanced, centered way.

But for today, take a moment to appreciate the self-awareness and emotional intelligence you've cultivated.

Remember: *You can't control the triggers, but you can always control how you respond to them. Managing your triggers is about choosing your emotional state with intention and care.*

DAY 14: THE GRATITUDE MINDSET

Welcome to Day 14. Over the past two weeks, you've done the deep inner work of building resilience, trust, and self-compassion.

Today, we shift focus to a practice that can become the emotional anchor of your journey—*gratitude*.

Gratitude is one of the simplest yet most powerful tools for transforming your mindset and emotional state. It invites you to notice the small blessings, the subtle beauty, and the moments of joy that often get overlooked in the rush of everyday life.

In a world that constantly pushes us to think about what's missing or what we need to strive for, gratitude pulls you back to what's already here. It reminds you that, in many ways, you are already enough, already abundant, already fulfilled.

When you practice gratitude, you shift your focus from scarcity to abundance. This practice doesn't mean ignoring challenges or denying difficulties, but rather acknowledging that even in tough moments, there are things—however small—that can bring light, warmth, and strength into your life.

Today, we'll explore the profound impact of gratitude on emotional resilience, and you'll start a daily gratitude practice that can rewire your mindset for joy and balance.

What is Gratitude?

Gratitude is the conscious act of recognizing and appreciating the goodness in your life.

It's about taking a moment to pause and acknowledge what's going well, what brings you peace, or what you cherish—no matter how fleeting or small it may seem.

Gratitude is often described as a shift in perspective:

- **From lack to abundance**: Rather than focusing on what you don't have, gratitude centers your attention on the richness already present in your life.
- **From future to present**: Gratitude grounds you in the present moment, allowing you to savor the here and now without constantly striving for more.
- **From comparison to appreciation**: Instead of comparing your journey to others, gratitude fosters contentment with where you are and the unique path you're on.

Gratitude isn't about pretending that everything is perfect. It's about noticing that, even when life is hard, there are moments of grace, connection, and joy that you can be thankful for.

Whether it's the kindness of a friend, the beauty of nature, or a simple cup of tea, gratitude opens your heart to the abundance that exists in every moment.

The Power of Gratitude on Emotional Resilience

Gratitude is more than a feel-good practice—it's a scientifically backed tool for enhancing emotional resilience. When you practice gratitude regularly, you build the emotional muscles needed to handle life's ups and downs with more grace and balance.

Gratitude helps you focus on what's working, what's nourishing, and what's beautiful, which can offer much-needed perspective during difficult times.

Here's how gratitude builds emotional resilience:

- **It fosters a positive mindset**: Gratitude helps you notice and appreciate the good things in your life, no matter how small. This shift in perspective creates a more positive outlook, making it easier to face challenges with a solution-focused attitude.
- **It reduces stress**: Studies have shown that gratitude lowers stress levels by decreasing cortisol, the stress hormone. When you focus on what you're thankful for, your body and mind relax, and you're less likely to be overwhelmed by external pressures.
- **It creates emotional grounding**: Gratitude roots you in the present moment, offering an emotional anchor during times of uncertainty or difficulty. When you pause to reflect on what's going well, you're less likely to spiral into fear or anxiety.
- **It builds hope and optimism**: By consistently noticing the good in your life, gratitude fosters a sense of hope. Even when things don't go as planned, gratitude reminds you that there are still things to appreciate and that brighter moments lie ahead.

Practicing gratitude doesn't magically erase difficulties, but it does help you build a mindset that's more resilient, more focused on growth, and more appreciative of life's everyday gifts.

The Science of Gratitude

Gratitude isn't just a spiritual or philosophical concept—it's rooted in science. Neuroscientific research shows that practicing gratitude can literally rewire your brain, helping you to focus more on the positive aspects of life and less on the negative.

Here's how gratitude works on a neurological level:

- **Neuroplasticity**: Regularly practicing gratitude strengthens the neural pathways associated with positive thinking. Over time, your brain becomes better at recognizing and savoring positive experiences.
- **Boosted serotonin and dopamine**: Gratitude increases levels of the "feel-good" neurotransmitters, serotonin and dopamine, which are key to maintaining a balanced mood and a sense of well-being.
- **Improved emotional regulation**: Gratitude enhances the prefrontal cortex—the part of the brain responsible for decision-making and emotional regulation. This means you're better able to manage emotional reactions and respond to life's challenges in a more balanced way.

When you make gratitude a daily practice, you're not just influencing your mindset—you're reshaping your brain to experience more joy, peace, and emotional stability.

The Daily Practice of Gratitude

The power of gratitude lies in its consistency. While it's easy to feel grateful on good days, the real growth comes when you practice it during difficult times.

This consistency builds emotional strength and helps you maintain perspective, even in the midst of challenges.

Here's how to incorporate gratitude into your daily life:

1. **Start small**: Begin by noticing small things you're grateful for throughout your day—a friendly smile, a hot cup of coffee, or a moment of peace in a busy schedule. These small moments are just as important as the big ones.
2. **Create a gratitude ritual**: Whether it's writing in a journal before bed or taking a few moments each

morning to reflect, establish a consistent time each day for your gratitude practice. Consistency is key to seeing the lasting benefits of gratitude.
3. **Be specific**: Instead of writing general things like "I'm grateful for my family," get specific. Write about a particular conversation, gesture, or moment that made you feel loved or appreciated. This specificity makes your gratitude practice more meaningful.
4. **Practice mindful gratitude**: Throughout your day, pause when something positive happens and take a moment to truly savor it. Mindful gratitude helps you stay present and deepen your appreciation for life's small pleasures.
5. **Express gratitude to others**: Sharing your gratitude with the people in your life strengthens relationships and spreads positivity. Take time to thank a friend, family member, or colleague. Not only will it brighten their day, but it will also deepen your connection.

Gratitude is a practice, and like any practice, it requires commitment. The more you engage with gratitude, the more you'll notice its ripple effects in your life, bringing more joy, emotional balance, and a sense of contentment.

Exercise: Start a Daily Gratitude Journal

Today's exercise is designed to help you develop a daily gratitude practice.

By keeping a gratitude journal, you'll train your mind to focus on the positive aspects of your day, creating a habit that will enhance your emotional resilience over time.

Step 1: Choose Your Journal

Find a journal that you enjoy writing in. It doesn't have to be elaborate—a simple notebook will do.

The important thing is that it feels like a space where you can reflect and express your thoughts comfortably.

Step 2: Write Down Three Things You're Grateful For

At the end of each day, take five minutes to write down three things you're grateful for. They don't have to be major accomplishments or life-changing events.

In fact, some of the most powerful moments of gratitude come from the small, everyday blessings.

Here are some prompts to help you reflect:

- **What went well today?**
- **Who made you smile or feel supported?**
- **What small moment brought you joy or peace?**
- **What is something in your daily routine that you often take for granted but are thankful for?**

Example:

- *I'm grateful for the peaceful morning walk I took today—it helped me clear my mind.*
- *I'm thankful for the encouraging text message I received from my friend. It made me feel valued and supported.*
- *I'm grateful for the cup of tea I had this evening—it brought me a moment of calm after a busy day.*

Step 3: Reflect on the Impact

After writing your gratitude list, take a moment to reflect on how it feels to focus on the positive aspects of your day. Notice if your mood shifts as you reflect on what went well.

This small shift in focus can create a ripple effect of positivity in your mindset, helping you feel more grounded and emotionally balanced.

Reflection on the Exercise

How did it feel to write down the things you're grateful for today? Did you notice a change in how you viewed your day? This simple practice of daily gratitude, when done consistently, can have profound effects on your emotional resilience and overall mindset.

Each time you write in your gratitude journal, you're training your brain to focus on abundance and positivity, helping you navigate life with greater joy and grace.

Takeaway

Today, you embraced the transformative power of gratitude. By starting a daily gratitude practice, you're cultivating a mindset that focuses on abundance, joy, and the positive aspects of your life.

Gratitude doesn't eliminate challenges, but it does help you build the emotional strength to see the good, even in hard times. It rewires your brain for resilience and helps you stay grounded in the present.

As you continue this journey, remember that gratitude is a practice that grows with time.

The more you engage with it, the more naturally you'll begin to notice the small, beautiful moments in your day, and the more balanced and content you'll feel.

Tomorrow, we'll explore how to stay centered and grounded during times of stress and uncertainty.

But for today, take a moment to reflect on the power of gratitude and the gifts that already surround you.

Remember: *Gratitude is the practice of finding joy in the present. By focusing on what's good in your life, you cultivate emotional resilience, contentment, and a deeper connection to the abundance that's already within you.*

PART 3: BECOMING YOUR MOST AUTHENTIC SELF

Week 3: Embodying Self-Connection and Inner Strength

DAY 15: RECONNECTING WITH YOUR INNER CHILD

Welcome to Day 15. As we begin the final week of your journey, the focus shifts from internal discovery to *embodying* everything you've learned.

You've been building emotional resilience, self-awareness, and self-compassion—and now it's time to fully embrace your most authentic self.

To do this, we're diving into one of the most transformative and healing practices: *reconnecting with your inner child.*

Your inner child is the part of you that carries the essence of your earliest experiences—your first moments of joy, creativity, love, and curiosity. It's also the part of you that holds any unhealed wounds, unmet needs, and unresolved feelings from your past.

These experiences continue to shape your life today in ways that can affect your self-connection, your relationships, and your sense of worth.

Reconnecting with your inner child is about healing those early emotional wounds and reclaiming the sense of playfulness, creativity, and wonder that is essential to who you are. It's about acknowledging the vulnerable, sensitive parts of yourself that may have been ignored or silenced over the years, and offering them the love and care they needed then—and still need now.

Why Reconnecting with Your Inner Child Matters

Your inner child is the gateway to your most authentic self. This part of you was present long before you learned how to wear masks, before societal expectations, before you began comparing yourself to others.

Your inner child holds the key to your original, unfiltered self—the version of you that simply *is*, without fear, shame, or doubt.

But as life progresses, we often push that part of ourselves aside. We learn to prioritize productivity over play, achievement over creativity, and perfection over authenticity. As a result, many of us lose touch with the joy and spontaneity we experienced as children.

Worse, unhealed wounds from childhood—whether from rejection, criticism, or unmet emotional needs—continue to affect us, showing up in our adult lives as fears, insecurities, or emotional blocks.

Here's why reconnecting with your inner child is crucial:

- **It heals past wounds**: By acknowledging and caring for your inner child, you can address unresolved emotions and heal old wounds that still influence your adult self. You offer love and protection to the part of you that may have felt abandoned or misunderstood.
- **It unlocks joy and creativity**: Your inner child is naturally curious, playful, and creative. Reconnecting with them helps you tap into these qualities, bringing more fun, imagination, and joy into your daily life.
- **It deepens your authenticity**: When you reconnect with your inner child, you strip away the layers of fear and conditioning that have kept you from expressing your

true self. This allows you to live more authentically and in alignment with your core values.

Healing your inner child is not about blaming others or dwelling on the past. Instead, it's about understanding the impact of your early experiences and offering yourself the care and love you may not have received at the time.

This process creates space for growth, healing, and greater self-connection, helping you step into your most authentic self.

Recognizing the Voice of Your Inner Child

Your inner child still exists within you. They often make themselves known in subtle ways—through your emotional reactions, your instincts, and your deeply held desires or fears. However, over time, you may have learned to quiet this voice, especially if childhood wounds or unmet needs were painful to confront.

Here are some ways your inner child might be showing up in your life:

- **Emotional reactions**: Have you ever noticed that certain situations or interactions provoke an intense emotional response that feels out of proportion to the event? Often, these reactions stem from unresolved emotions your inner child is still carrying.
- **Yearning for safety or approval**: If you find yourself constantly seeking validation or approval from others, this may reflect your inner child's unmet need for love, protection, or acknowledgment.
- **Difficulty with play or relaxation**: If you struggle to allow yourself moments of play, creativity, or relaxation without feeling guilty, your inner child may be calling out

for permission to experience joy and freedom.
- **Perfectionism or fear of failure**: If you fear making mistakes or feel the need to be perfect, this could be rooted in your inner child's need to feel safe and accepted, especially in environments where mistakes were met with criticism.

Recognizing when your inner child is speaking can help you pause and respond with compassion.

Instead of dismissing or suppressing those feelings, you can begin to meet the needs of your inner child in a healthy, supportive way.

Healing Your Inner Child

Healing your inner child is a gentle process that requires patience and compassion. It's about giving your inner child the love, protection, and validation they needed at critical moments in your past—and still need today.

You're essentially re-parenting yourself, offering the care and understanding that may have been lacking when you were younger.

Here's what healing your inner child involves:

- **Acknowledging their emotions**: Allow your inner child to express their feelings without judgment. Whether it's fear, anger, sadness, or confusion, validate those emotions and let them know it's okay to feel whatever they're feeling.
- **Offering love and protection**: Reassure your inner child that they are safe now, and that you are here to protect them. Let them know that they are loved and that they no longer have to face challenges alone.
- **Encouraging play and creativity**: Invite your inner child to experience joy, fun, and creativity again. Give yourself permission to play, to imagine, to explore—without worrying about being "productive" or perfect.

Healing your inner child doesn't mean you have to revisit every painful memory from the past. It's about offering compassion and understanding to the parts of yourself that are still hurting, while inviting joy and creativity back into your life.

Exercise: Write a Letter to Your Inner Child

Today's exercise is about reconnecting with and healing your inner child by writing them a letter.

This is a powerful way to acknowledge your younger self's experiences, offer them love and protection, and reassure them that they are seen, valued, and safe.

Step 1: Find a Quiet Space

Before you begin, find a quiet space where you feel safe and comfortable. This is a moment of self-connection, so give yourself the privacy and time to fully engage with the process.

Take a few deep breaths, and allow yourself to settle into a calm state.

Step 2: Visualize Your Inner Child

Close your eyes and imagine yourself as a child. Picture the younger version of you—what did they look like? What were they feeling? Try to visualize specific memories or moments from your childhood.

Now, imagine your inner child standing in front of you, looking to you for comfort, love, or guidance.

Step 3: Write the Letter

Now, begin writing your letter. Speak directly to your inner child, offering them the words they may have needed but never received.

This letter is a chance to give your inner child the love, validation, and protection that was missing in their life. Let them know that they are worthy of love and that they are safe now.

Here are some prompts to guide your letter:

- **Acknowledge their experiences**: "I know you felt scared when..." or "I see that you struggled with feeling..."
- **Offer love and reassurance**: "You are so loved, just as you are." or "I'm here now to protect you."
- **Encourage joy and creativity**: "It's okay to play and have fun." or "You are free to be creative and express yourself without fear."

Example: *"Dear [Your Name],*

I see you, and I know how hard things were for you. I remember the times when you felt invisible or unworthy, and I want you to know that those feelings were valid. But I'm here now, and I want you to know that you are more than enough. You are so deeply loved, just as you are. You don't have to earn love or be perfect to deserve it—you are worthy simply because you exist.

I will protect you. I will be the one to take care of you when things feel overwhelming, and I will make sure you always feel safe and loved. You are free to play, to be joyful, and to express yourself however you want. It's okay to make mistakes, and it's okay to just be. I'm proud of you, and I love you."

Step 4: Reflect on the Process

Once you've finished your letter, take a few moments to reflect on how the process felt. Did writing the letter bring up any emotions or memories? How did it feel to offer love and protection to your inner child?

Allow yourself to sit with these feelings without judgment.

Reflection on the Exercise

How did it feel to reconnect with your inner child through writing? Did you experience any moments of clarity, emotion, or healing? This letter is a powerful way to begin the process of healing your inner child and offering them the love and care they've always needed.

Remember, this connection is ongoing, and you can return to this practice whenever you feel the need to reconnect with your authentic self.

Takeaway

Today, you took a brave and compassionate step toward healing your inner child. By offering love, protection, and validation, you've begun to address the wounds of the past and create a deeper connection with the most authentic version of yourself.

This process opens the door to more creativity, joy, and emotional freedom.

As you continue this journey, keep listening to your inner child. Offer them care, play, and understanding, and you'll find that the more you nurture this part of yourself, the more aligned and whole you'll feel.

Tomorrow, we'll explore the power of self-expression and how it plays a role in living as your most authentic self.

But for today, take a moment to appreciate the healing you've started and the emotional strength you're building.

Remember: *Your inner child is the heart of your authenticity. By healing and reconnecting with them, you unlock joy, creativity, and the freedom to be your truest self.*

DAY 16: LIVING WITH PURPOSE

Welcome to Day 16. In this final week of becoming your most authentic self, we focus on one of the most profound aspects of personal growth: *living with purpose.*

Throughout this journey, you've connected with your inner self, built emotional resilience, and embraced self-compassion.

Now, it's time to align everything you've learned with something larger—your sense of purpose.

Living with purpose means more than setting goals or achieving success. It's about aligning your daily actions with the things that matter most to you.

When you live with purpose, you're not just going through the motions of life; you're actively choosing to engage with the world in ways that reflect your deepest values and passions.

Purpose brings clarity, fulfillment, and direction to your life, and it gives meaning to your everyday experiences.

Finding your purpose can feel like a big task, but it doesn't need to be overwhelming. Purpose isn't a distant, abstract idea that you have to search for—it's something that's already within you, waiting to be uncovered.

Today, we'll explore how to connect with your purpose and how living with it can guide your actions, relationships, and decisions in a way that feels true to who you are.

What Does It Mean to Live with Purpose?

Living with purpose is the act of aligning your choices, actions, and lifestyle with what matters most to you. It's about living intentionally, rather than letting life happen to you.

Whether in your career, relationships, or personal growth, living with purpose means consistently acting in ways that reflect your values, passions, and desires.

Here's how purpose shows up in daily life:

- **Clarity in your actions**: When you live with purpose, you don't feel pulled in a thousand directions. Your actions are guided by a deeper sense of meaning, making it easier to say "yes" to what aligns with your purpose and "no" to what doesn't.
- **Alignment with your values**: Purpose is grounded in your core values—the principles that matter most to you. Living with purpose means that your decisions reflect those values, whether it's integrity, connection, growth, or creativity.
- **Passion in your pursuits**: Purpose fuels your passion. It makes you excited to wake up each day and engage with the world, because your actions are tied to something meaningful. This sense of passion and enthusiasm brings energy and fulfillment to your daily life.
- **Meaning in the everyday**: Purpose transforms even ordinary moments into opportunities for growth and connection. When you're living with purpose, everything from how you interact with loved ones to how you approach challenges can be seen through the lens of meaning.

Living with purpose isn't just about what you do; it's about how and why you do it. It's the difference between going through life on autopilot and waking up every day feeling connected to something bigger than yourself.

The Importance of Purpose in Authenticity

Living with purpose is essential to becoming your most authentic self. Without a sense of purpose, it's easy to feel lost, unfulfilled, or out of alignment with your true desires.

Purpose serves as a compass, guiding you toward decisions that are in line with your authentic self rather than decisions driven by external pressures or societal expectations.

Here's why living with purpose is key to authenticity:

- **It creates alignment between who you are and what you do**: Authenticity comes from being true to yourself in every area of your life. When you live with purpose, your actions and decisions reflect your core values, making you feel more connected to your authentic self.
- **It deepens your self-awareness**: Purpose isn't something that comes from outside of you. It's an expression of your innermost desires, passions, and values. As you live with purpose, you continually check in with yourself, ensuring that your choices are in line with who you truly are.
- **It fosters emotional resilience**: Purpose provides a sense of direction and meaning, which can help you stay grounded even during difficult times. When you know why you're doing something, you're more likely to push through challenges with grace and resilience.
- **It enhances fulfillment**: A purposeful life is a fulfilling life. When your actions are aligned with your purpose, you experience a deeper sense of satisfaction because you know you're living in a way that is true to your values.

Living with purpose allows you to fully embody who you are. It gives you the courage to make decisions that reflect your truth and the confidence to live life on your own terms.

Finding Your Purpose

One of the biggest misconceptions about purpose is that it's something you have to discover through some grand revelation.

But in reality, purpose is more often uncovered gradually—through reflection, exploration, and alignment with your values and passions.

Here are some signs that point to your purpose:

- **What lights you up**: Purpose is often connected to the things that ignite your passion. What activities make you feel excited, energized, and fully engaged? These are clues to what brings meaning and joy to your life.
- **What challenges you deeply**: Purpose can also be found in the challenges that move you emotionally. Is there a cause or issue that you care about so deeply it drives you to act? Your purpose might live at the intersection of passion and challenge.
- **Where you feel a sense of contribution**: Purpose often involves a sense of contribution—whether to your community, loved ones, or a cause you care about. Think about the ways you want to give back or make a difference. These desires can help point you toward your purpose.
- **What aligns with your values**: Purpose is deeply tied to your core values. Reflect on the principles that guide your life. Are they centered on creativity, kindness, connection, or justice? Purpose comes from living in alignment with these values.

Your purpose doesn't have to be grand or world-changing. It might be as simple as living in a way that brings joy and peace to yourself and those around you.

The key is to listen to your inner voice and align your life with the things that matter most to you.

Exercise: Discovering Your Life's Purpose

Today's exercise will guide you through a reflective process to help you explore your life's purpose. By answering these questions, you'll gain clarity on what gives your life meaning and how you can align your actions with your true self.

Step 1: Reflect on Your Passions and Joys

Start by thinking about the things that bring you the most joy and fulfillment. These are often clues to your purpose.

Here are some questions to guide your reflection:

- **What activities make you feel most alive?**
  Consider the moments when you feel fully present and engaged in life. What are you doing? Who are you with? What about those moments brings you joy?
- **When do you feel most connected to yourself?**
  Think about the times when you feel a deep connection to your true self—when you're not performing for anyone or trying to meet external expectations. What are you doing during these moments? How can you create more of them in your life?

Step 2: Identify Your Core Values

Next, reflect on your core values. These are the principles that guide your actions and shape your sense of purpose.

Here are some prompts to help you identify your values:

- **What's most important to you in life?**
  Consider what you value most—whether it's integrity, creativity, connection, or growth. These values will help guide you toward your purpose.
- **What do you admire in others?**

Think about the qualities you admire in the people around you. Often, the things we admire in others reflect our own values. What does this tell you about what's most important to you?

Step 3: Connect Passion to Purpose

Now that you've reflected on your passions and values, think about how they can come together to create a sense of purpose in your life.

Here are some guiding questions:

- **How can you combine your passions and values?**
  Reflect on how the things that bring you joy and the values that matter most to you can come together. For example, if you're passionate about creativity and value connection, perhaps your purpose is to use creativity to bring people together.
- **What contribution do you want to make?**
  Think about how your passions and values can be used to make a positive contribution—whether in your community, your relationships, or your personal growth.

Step 4: Envision a Purposeful Life

Finally, imagine what your life would look like if you were fully living with purpose. Picture your daily actions aligning with your values and passions.

Here are some questions to guide your vision:

- **How would your life change if you lived with purpose every day?**
  Think about the small, everyday changes you could make to bring more meaning and alignment to your life.
- **What legacy do you want to leave behind?**
  Imagine looking back on your life. What do you hope to have accomplished? What impact do you want to leave on the people around you or the world?

Reflection on the Exercise

How did it feel to reflect on your life's purpose? Were there any moments of clarity or insight? Remember, purpose is not a destination but a journey.

The more you align your actions with your values and passions, the more purposeful your life will become.

Takeaway

Today, you took a meaningful step toward living with purpose. By reflecting on your passions, values, and the contributions you want to make, you've gained clarity on what truly matters to you.

Living with purpose is not about achieving a singular goal—it's about aligning your actions, decisions, and daily life with what brings you the most fulfillment and meaning.

As you move forward, continue to explore how you can live with greater intention. Purpose is found in the small, daily choices you make, and every moment is an opportunity to live in alignment with your true self.

Tomorrow, we'll focus on turning your purpose into actionable steps that will help you continue living authentically and meaningfully.

But for today, take a moment to appreciate the clarity you've gained and the purpose that's already within you.

Remember: *Living with purpose is about aligning your everyday actions with your values and passions. When you live with purpose, you live with clarity, fulfillment, and a deeper connection to your authentic self.*

DAY 17: EXPRESSING YOUR TRUE SELF

Welcome to Day 17. As you continue to step into your most authentic self, today's focus is on one of the most empowering and liberating aspects of self-connection: *authentic self-expression*.

Authentic self-expression is about more than just sharing your thoughts or opinions—it's about giving voice to the deepest parts of yourself. It's about finding ways to express the emotions, experiences, and inner truths that make you *you*.

Whether through writing, art, movement, or even how you interact with the world, authentic self-expression allows you to communicate the essence of who you are.

This can be a vulnerable process, and for many of us, it comes with challenges. We may worry about judgment, fear rejection, or struggle with feeling like our voice isn't important.

However, the act of expressing your true self is one of the most powerful ways to connect more deeply with yourself and with others. When you speak, create, or live from a place of authenticity, you honor your inner world, strengthen your emotional resilience, and inspire those around you to do the same.

Today, we'll explore how to tap into this authentic self-expression, how to overcome the fears that might hold you back, and how to make creative expression a part of your life in ways that feel meaningful and aligned with who you truly are.

What is Authentic Self-Expression?

Authentic self-expression is the act of communicating your inner experiences, thoughts, emotions, and values in a way that feels true to you. It's about expressing who you *really* are, without filtering or censoring yourself to fit the expectations of others.

This could take the form of words, art, music, movement, or even the way you show up in your daily life.

Here's what authentic self-expression looks like:

- **Being true to your emotions**: Rather than hiding or suppressing what you feel, authentic self-expression allows you to give voice to your emotions. It could be as simple as journaling about your day or as complex as creating a work of art that captures your emotional landscape.
- **Speaking from your heart**: Whether you're engaging in a conversation, writing, or performing, speaking from your heart means communicating in a way that reflects your true thoughts and beliefs. It's about being honest and vulnerable, even when it feels uncomfortable.
- **Tapping into creativity**: Authentic expression often involves creativity—whether it's painting, dancing, writing, or another form of art. Creative expression gives you the freedom to explore and communicate your inner world without the constraints of language or logic.
- **Living authentically**: Self-expression isn't just about what you say or create—it's about how you live. Living authentically means aligning your actions, choices, and lifestyle with your true values and desires.

Self-expression is a deeply personal practice. There's no "right" way to do it. What matters is that you allow yourself the freedom to express what's inside, without holding back or worrying about how it will be received.

The more you practice expressing your true self, the more connected you'll feel to your inner world.

Why Authentic Self-Expression is Key to Self-Connection

At its core, authentic self-expression is about *connection*. It's about bridging the gap between your inner world and how you present yourself to the outer world.

For many of us, this gap can feel wide. We may hide parts of ourselves, downplay our emotions, or hold back our thoughts out of fear of being judged or misunderstood.

But when you express your true self, you strengthen your connection to who you are at your core. You create space to be seen, heard, and understood—first by yourself, and then by others.

Authentic self-expression allows you to show up fully in your life, without wearing a mask or pretending to be someone you're not.

Here's why self-expression is vital to self-connection:

- **It enhances self-awareness**: When you express yourself authentically, you become more aware of your thoughts, feelings, and experiences. Whether through journaling, talking with a friend, or creating art, self-expression helps you process your emotions and gain clarity about what's happening inside.
- **It prevents emotional suppression**: Suppressing your emotions can lead to emotional buildup, which may manifest as stress, anxiety, or frustration. Authentic self-expression gives you a healthy outlet to release and process what you're feeling, which helps you maintain emotional balance.

- **It nurtures creativity and play**: Creativity is a powerful tool for self-expression. Whether through painting, writing, or movement, creativity allows you to explore and communicate your inner experiences in ways that feel joyful, playful, and free.
- **It deepens connections with others**: Authentic expression fosters deeper relationships. When you express yourself vulnerably and honestly, you invite others to see the real you, creating space for more meaningful and authentic connections.

Self-expression is a way to honor your inner voice. It's an opportunity to listen to what's inside and allow that voice to come forward, without fear of judgment.

This process is key to living in alignment with your true self.

Overcoming the Fear of Vulnerability

For many of us, the idea of expressing our true self can feel scary. There's often a fear of vulnerability—of being judged, rejected, or misunderstood.

You might worry that if you share your innermost thoughts, feelings, or creative work, others won't accept or understand you.

But vulnerability is at the heart of authentic self-expression. To express yourself fully, you have to be willing to be seen—flaws, imperfections, and all.

This is what makes self-expression so powerful. When you allow yourself to be vulnerable, you're not only honoring your truth, but you're also building resilience and strength in the process.

Here's how you can overcome the fear of vulnerability in self-expression:

- **Acknowledge the fear**: It's okay to feel scared. Vulnerability is uncomfortable because it exposes parts of yourself that you might usually protect. Acknowledge the fear without letting it control you.
- **Start small**: You don't have to start by sharing your deepest thoughts with the world. Begin with small acts of expression—journal privately, share a thought with a trusted friend, or create art that only you will see. Over time, you'll build the confidence to express yourself more fully.
- **Remember your voice matters**: It's easy to fall into the trap of thinking your voice isn't important or that what you have to say doesn't matter. But your voice *does* matter. Expressing your inner world is a powerful act of self-connection and self-respect.
- **Let go of perfection**: Authentic expression isn't about being perfect or polished—it's about being real. Allow yourself to be messy, imperfect, and human. The beauty of self-expression lies in its honesty, not in its perfection.

By embracing vulnerability, you create space for deeper self-connection and growth. The more you practice, the more confident you'll become in expressing your true self without fear.

The Many Forms of Self-Expression

Authentic self-expression can take many different forms, and the best way to express yourself depends on what resonates with you. You might be someone who expresses themselves through words, or you may feel more connected to your inner world through visual art, music, or movement. The key is to find the form of expression that feels most aligned with your natural way of being.

Here are some ways you can explore authentic self-expression:

- **Writing**: Whether it's journaling, poetry, or storytelling, writing allows you to put your thoughts and emotions into words. Writing can be a deeply therapeutic way to clarify your feelings and express your inner world.
- **Art**: Painting, drawing, or creating something visual can help you express emotions and ideas that might be difficult to put into words. Art gives you the freedom to explore your creativity and communicate your feelings in a way that feels abstract or symbolic.
- **Movement**: Dance, yoga, or other forms of movement allow you to connect with your body and express yourself physically. Movement can be a powerful way to release emotions, tap into your energy, and feel more present in your body.
- **Music**: Playing an instrument, singing, or simply listening to music that resonates with you can be a profound form of self-expression. Music has the ability to evoke and express emotions that words alone cannot capture.
- **Conversation**: Engaging in meaningful, open conversations with trusted friends or loved ones is another form of self-expression. Sharing your thoughts and feelings in a safe space allows you to communicate authentically and connect with others on a deeper level.

There's no right or wrong way to express yourself.

The most important thing is that you find a form of expression that feels true to you, and that allows you to connect with your inner self in an authentic and meaningful way.

Exercise: Create Something That Expresses Your Inner World

Today's exercise is an invitation to express your true self through creativity. You'll choose a medium—whether it's writing, art, movement, or another creative outlet—and create something that reflects your inner world.

This exercise is about giving voice to your inner thoughts, feelings, and experiences in a way that feels authentic and freeing.

Step 1: Choose Your Medium

Begin by deciding how you'd like to express yourself today. Do you feel drawn to writing, painting, music, or movement?

Choose the form of expression that feels most aligned with your current emotional state and energy.

Step 2: Set the Intention to Be Authentic

Before you begin, set the intention to express yourself authentically.

Remind yourself that this exercise is not about creating something "perfect" or impressive—it's about being true to your inner experience. Give yourself permission to be messy, vulnerable, and real.

Step 3: Create Without Overthinking

Now, let your creativity flow. Whether you're writing, painting, or dancing, allow your inner thoughts, emotions, and experiences to guide the process.

Don't worry about how it will look or sound—focus on expressing what's inside you.

Here are some prompts to guide your creation:

- **What am I feeling right now, and how can I express it?**
  Tune into your emotional state and let it shape your creative expression. If you're feeling joy, create something that reflects that. If you're feeling introspective, allow that to guide your work.
- **What part of myself do I want to express?**
  Reflect on whether there's a part of yourself—an emotion,

thought, or experience—that you've been holding back. Use this exercise as an opportunity to give that part of yourself a voice.

- **What does my inner world look like?**
Imagine your inner world as a landscape, a color, or a scene. How can you bring that inner vision to life through your chosen medium?

Step 4: Reflect on the Process

Once you've finished creating, take a moment to reflect on how the process felt. Did any emotions or insights arise while you were expressing yourself? How did it feel to give voice to your inner world?

Allow yourself to sit with these reflections without judgment.

Reflection on the Exercise

How did it feel to create something that expressed your inner world? Did you notice any new emotions, thoughts, or insights emerge during the process?

Authentic self-expression is a powerful tool for deepening your connection to yourself, and each time you engage in it, you strengthen your sense of authenticity and alignment with your true self.

Takeaway

Today, you embraced the power of authentic self-expression. By creating something that reflected your inner world, you honored your emotions, thoughts, and experiences in a way that felt true to you.

This is a powerful practice that not only deepens your self-connection but also brings more creativity, joy, and authenticity into your life.

As you move forward, continue to explore different forms of self-expression. Whether through writing, art, music, or conversation, allow yourself the freedom to express your true self in ways that feel meaningful and aligned with who you are.

Tomorrow, we'll dive deeper into integrating all the practices we've explored so far into your daily life. But for today, take a moment to celebrate the beauty and power of your authentic voice.

Remember: *Authentic self-expression is an act of courage and self-love. When you express your true self, you honor your inner world and deepen your connection to who you truly are.*

DAY 18: EMBRACING IMPERFECTIONS

Welcome to Day 18. As you near the end of this journey to self-connection and authenticity, today's focus is on something that lies at the heart of true self-acceptance: *embracing your imperfections.*

We live in a world that constantly pushes the idea that perfection equals worthiness. From social media to career expectations to relationships, we are bombarded with images and messages that tell us we must be flawless to be valuable, loved, or successful.

But chasing perfection is like chasing the horizon—it's always out of reach. The more we strive for it, the further away we feel from truly accepting ourselves.

Real self-acceptance is not about becoming "perfect"; it's about embracing *all* of who you are, including your flaws, quirks, and imperfections. These so-called imperfections are not weaknesses or things to hide—they are what make you beautifully unique and real. By embracing them, you open yourself to deeper self-compassion, resilience, and authenticity.

Today, we'll explore how to let go of the impossible pursuit of perfection and learn to love the parts of yourself that make you who you are.

The Beauty of Imperfection

Imperfection is not the opposite of beauty; it's an essential part of it. Think about the natural world—whether it's the curve of a tree branch, the irregular shape of a seashell, or the unpredictable patterns in the clouds, nature doesn't conform to rigid standards of symmetry or perfection.

It is *because* of its flaws and irregularities that nature is breathtakingly beautiful.

The same is true for people. Perfection is an illusion, but the beauty of your humanity lies in your imperfections. They are what make you real, what give you depth, and what tell the story of your unique journey.

Your imperfections are a testament to your growth, your struggles, your resilience, and your evolution. When you learn to embrace them, you're not just accepting your flaws—you're celebrating the complexity and richness of your life.

Here's why your imperfections are beautiful:

- **They tell your story**: Each imperfection, whether it's a physical feature, a personality trait, or an emotional quirk, is part of your unique story. These so-called flaws are the marks of your experiences, struggles, and growth. They show where you've been and how you've evolved.
- **They make you relatable**: Perfection creates distance, while imperfection creates connection. When you embrace your flaws, you allow others to see the real, unpolished version of you. This vulnerability builds trust and creates more authentic relationships because it lets others know it's okay to be imperfect, too.
- **They foster growth**: Your imperfections are not just things to tolerate—they are opportunities for learning and growth. They highlight the areas of your life where you've had to stretch, adapt, and build resilience. Each flaw teaches you something about yourself, about life, and about how to move forward with strength.

Embracing imperfection is about shifting your perspective. Instead of seeing your flaws as things that need fixing, start seeing them as beautiful, irreplaceable parts of your story. They make you *you*.

The Harm of Perfectionism

Many of us fall into the trap of perfectionism, believing that if we could just be perfect, then we would be happy, loved, or successful. But perfectionism is a thief of joy. It keeps you constantly striving, never feeling good enough, and always critical of yourself. Rather than making you better, perfectionism actually limits your ability to live freely and authentically.

Perfectionism leads to:

- **Self-criticism**: Perfectionism fuels a harsh inner voice that constantly points out where you're falling short. You become your own worst critic, unable to appreciate your accomplishments because you're focused on where you didn't measure up.
- **Fear of failure**: The fear of making mistakes or being judged for not being perfect can paralyze you. It can stop you from taking risks, trying new things, or stepping outside your comfort zone. You may find yourself avoiding opportunities because you're afraid of not being perfect.
- **Burnout**: The pursuit of perfection is exhausting. Trying to meet impossible standards—whether at work, in relationships, or even in self-improvement—leads to burnout. You can only push yourself so far before the stress and fatigue take a toll on your mental and emotional well-being.

The truth is, perfection is an illusion. No one is perfect, and no one needs to be.

By letting go of perfectionism, you free yourself to be fully present, to make mistakes, to learn, and to grow. It's in your imperfections that you find authenticity, connection, and peace.

Why Embracing Imperfections Is Key to Self-Acceptance

True self-acceptance means embracing all of who you are—including the parts of yourself that you've been taught to hide, fix, or change. When you accept your imperfections, you're no longer at war with yourself. You release the internal battle of trying to be someone you're not, and you allow yourself to *be*—flaws, quirks, and all.

Here's why embracing imperfections is essential to self-acceptance:

- **It builds self-compassion**: Accepting your imperfections means treating yourself with kindness, rather than harsh criticism. You stop beating yourself up for not being perfect and start seeing yourself with compassion and understanding. You acknowledge that being human means being imperfect, and that's okay.
- **It releases the need for external validation**: When you embrace your imperfections, you stop seeking approval from others to feel worthy. You no longer need external validation because you've found inner acceptance. This frees you from the pressure to conform to unrealistic standards and allows you to live authentically.
- **It fosters authenticity**: Perfectionism often requires you to wear a mask, hiding the parts of yourself that don't meet external standards. But when you embrace your imperfections, you allow yourself to show up fully as your true self, without the need to pretend or perform.
- **It encourages growth**: Imperfections are not roadblocks—they are stepping stones for growth. When you stop seeing them as flaws to fix and start viewing them

as opportunities for learning, you open yourself to new experiences, insights, and personal development.

Self-acceptance is not about being flawless; it's about loving yourself *despite* your flaws.

When you embrace your imperfections, you're no longer chasing an impossible version of yourself. Instead, you're grounding yourself in the beauty of who you truly are.

The Strength in Imperfections

One of the most empowering shifts you can make is to see your imperfections not as weaknesses, but as sources of strength. Each so-called flaw holds within it a lesson, a gift, or an opportunity for growth.

When you embrace your imperfections, you recognize that they are what make you resilient, adaptable, and unique.

Here's how your imperfections contribute to your strength:

- **They teach you resilience**: Every time you've stumbled, struggled, or faced a challenge, your imperfections have taught you how to bounce back. You've learned how to adapt, how to keep going even when things aren't perfect, and how to find strength in difficult situations.
- **They make you relatable and human**: Imperfections bring out your humanity. When you embrace them, you become more approachable and relatable. People connect with you not because you're perfect, but because you're real. Your imperfections create a bridge of empathy, helping you build deeper, more authentic relationships.
- **They inspire creativity**: Imperfections allow you to break free from rigid standards and explore new ways of being. Creativity often flourishes when you let go of the need for everything to be perfect. You can experiment, take risks, and find beauty in unexpected places because you're not bound by perfectionism.

- **They build emotional depth**: Your imperfections give you depth. They reveal the places where you've experienced pain, growth, and transformation. These experiences make you wiser, more empathetic, and more capable of navigating life's ups and downs.

Embracing your imperfections allows you to reclaim your power. Instead of seeing them as something that holds you back, you recognize that they are part of what makes you strong, resilient, and beautifully complex.

Exercise: Embrace Your Imperfections

Today's exercise is designed to help you embrace the parts of yourself that you may have been conditioned to hide or feel insecure about. Through reflection, you'll begin to see how your imperfections contribute to your uniqueness and strength.

Step 1: Make a List of Your Imperfections

Begin by listing the imperfections you've struggled with or felt self-conscious about. These could be aspects of your personality, physical traits, emotional tendencies, or past mistakes.

Be honest with yourself, and approach this list without judgment.

Here are some prompts to guide your list:

- What traits or behaviors have you been told to "fix"?
- What physical features have you felt insecure about?
- What mistakes or "failures" have shaped your sense of imperfection?
- Are there emotional tendencies (like sensitivity, anxiety, or impatience) that you've struggled to accept?

Step 2: Reflect on How Each Imperfection Contributes to Your Uniqueness

Now, take each item on your list and reflect on how it contributes to your uniqueness and strength. How have these imperfections shaped your experiences, relationships, or personal growth?

Here are some reflection prompts:

- **How has this imperfection taught you resilience?**
  Think about how overcoming challenges related to this trait has helped you grow stronger, more adaptable, or more compassionate.
- **How does this imperfection make you more empathetic or relatable?**
  Consider how embracing this flaw has helped you connect more deeply with others or allowed you to understand their struggles.
- **How does this imperfection make you beautifully unique?**
  Reflect on how this trait sets you apart and contributes to the richness of your personality and life experience.

Step 3: Reframe Each Imperfection as a Strength

For each imperfection, write a sentence that reframes it as a strength or a part of your uniqueness.

This exercise will help you shift your perspective from seeing these traits as flaws to recognizing their value.

Examples:

- *"My tendency to overthink has made me a careful, thoughtful decision-maker who considers all perspectives."*
- *"My scars remind me of the battles I've faced and the strength I've gained through adversity."*
- *"My sensitivity allows me to connect deeply with others and be attuned to their emotions."*

Reflection on the Exercise

How did it feel to reflect on your imperfections in this way? Did you notice any shifts in how you perceive these parts of yourself? Embracing your imperfections is a practice of self-love and acceptance.

ach of your so-called flaws contributes to your story, your strength, and your authenticity.

Takeaway

Today, you took a profound step toward embracing your imperfections and seeing them not as flaws but as integral parts of your uniqueness and strength.

Self-acceptance is not about being perfect—it's about loving yourself fully, just as you are. By embracing your imperfections, you free yourself from the impossible pursuit of perfection and open the door to greater compassion, resilience, and authenticity.

As you continue this journey, remember that your imperfections are not something to fix—they are something to celebrate. Each one is a piece of your story, a reflection of your humanity, and a testament to your growth.

Tomorrow, we'll focus on how to continue integrating these lessons into your daily life, so you can live authentically and confidently.

But for today, take a moment to honor the beauty of your imperfections and the strength they bring to your life.

Remember: *Perfection is an illusion. Your imperfections are what make you real, relatable, and beautifully unique. Embrace them, and you'll find freedom, strength, and true self-acceptance.*

DAY 19: ALIGNING WITH INTEGRITY

Welcome to Day 19. Today's focus is on a concept that forms the bedrock of self-connection and authenticity: *integrity*.

As you've worked to uncover your true self, build emotional resilience, and embrace your imperfections, it's now time to ensure that your daily actions, choices, and words align with your inner truth.

This alignment is the essence of integrity—living in a way that reflects your core values, and staying true to who you are, even when it's difficult.

Integrity is often spoken about in relation to honesty and morality, but it's much more than just being truthful with others. Integrity is about being truthful with yourself. It's about ensuring that your outer actions consistently reflect your inner values, and that there is no disconnect between what you believe, what you say, and how you behave.

When you live in alignment with your integrity, you feel a sense of coherence and peace because you're not betraying yourself to meet external expectations or social norms.

Living with integrity builds trust—trust in yourself and trust from others. It's how you strengthen your connection to your authentic self and cultivate meaningful, honest relationships.

But it's not always easy. There are moments when fear, convenience, or external pressures might tempt you to compromise on your values.

However, choosing integrity means choosing to live authentically and with intention, even when it's uncomfortable.

Today, we'll explore what it means to live in integrity, why it's essential for building self-trust and authenticity, and how to recognize and realign areas of your life where you may have fallen out of alignment.

Living with integrity is an ongoing practice, one that invites you to continuously reflect on your actions and ensure they're in harmony with your true self.

What Does It Mean to Live in Integrity?

Living in integrity means that your actions, decisions, and words are aligned with your deepest values and your authentic self. It's about being consistent in who you are across different areas of your life—whether in personal relationships, professional environments, or when you're alone with your thoughts.

Integrity isn't something you do just when it's convenient; it's the daily commitment to live according to what you know is right and true for you, even when it's challenging.

Here's what living in integrity looks like:

- **Alignment with your values**: Integrity begins with knowing what matters most to you. Whether your values include kindness, honesty, loyalty, courage, or creativity, living with integrity means ensuring that your actions reflect those values.
- **Consistency in your actions and words**: Integrity isn't just about what you believe internally; it's about how you express those beliefs externally. It means acting in ways that are consistent with your values, even when no one

is watching. It's about keeping your word and following through on your commitments to yourself and others.
- **Inner and outer harmony**: When you live with integrity, your inner world and outer world are aligned. There's no internal conflict because you're not pretending to be someone you're not or doing things that go against what you believe. This creates a sense of inner peace and clarity.
- **Acknowledgment of mistakes**: Living with integrity doesn't mean you're perfect or that you never make mistakes. It means being willing to acknowledge when you've stepped out of alignment with your values and taking action to correct it. Integrity includes taking responsibility for your actions and being honest with yourself when you need to make changes.

Living in integrity is about more than just following rules or meeting expectations. It's about being deeply in tune with your authentic self and ensuring that everything you do reflects who you truly are.

Why Integrity is Essential for Self-Connection

Integrity is foundational to a strong connection with yourself. When you consistently align your actions with your values, you build self-trust—a vital element of self-confidence and self-respect. Integrity helps you create a life that feels coherent, where you aren't pulled in different directions by external pressures or fears, but instead are guided by your own inner compass.

Here's why integrity is essential for self-connection:
- **It builds self-trust**: When you live in alignment with your values, you can trust yourself to make decisions that honor your truth. This self-trust is critical for feeling confident in your ability to navigate life. You know that, no matter

what, you will choose actions that reflect your authentic self.
- **It fosters inner peace**: There's a deep sense of peace that comes from living in alignment with your values. When your actions, words, and decisions reflect who you truly are, you no longer feel the internal conflict that comes from trying to please others or live up to external standards. You're grounded in your own truth.
- **It strengthens authenticity**: Integrity and authenticity are closely linked. When you live with integrity, you're living in a way that is true to who you are. This strengthens your sense of authenticity because you're no longer hiding parts of yourself or trying to fit into molds that don't suit you.
- **It enhances resilience**: Living with integrity gives you the strength to withstand external pressures because you're rooted in your values. When faced with difficult choices or challenges, you can rely on your integrity to guide you, knowing that acting in alignment with your values will lead you to the right outcome.

Living with integrity isn't always easy. There will be moments when the easier choice might be to compromise your values or act in ways that feel inauthentic.

But integrity is what grounds you. It allows you to trust yourself, even in those difficult moments, and to navigate life with a clear sense of purpose and truth.

The Consequences of Living Out of Integrity

At times, you may find yourself living out of alignment with your values. This can happen for a variety of reasons—fear, social pressure, convenience, or even a lack of clarity around your own beliefs.

However, living out of integrity often leads to internal

conflict and unease. You may feel disconnected from yourself or experience guilt, anxiety, or dissatisfaction without fully understanding why.

Here's what living out of integrity can look like:

- **Internal conflict**: When your actions don't align with your values, you may feel a sense of internal tension or discomfort. This could show up as unease, guilt, or a persistent feeling that something is "off." Living out of integrity creates a disconnect between who you are and how you're acting, leading to internal conflict.
- **Lack of self-trust**: When you regularly act out of alignment with your values, you may start to lose trust in yourself. You may second-guess your decisions or feel less confident in your ability to stay true to your beliefs. Over time, this erodes your sense of self-confidence and self-respect.
- **Inauthentic relationships**: Living out of integrity can also impact your relationships. When you're not being true to yourself, your relationships may feel shallow or inauthentic. You may find yourself engaging in people-pleasing behaviors or avoiding difficult conversations, leading to a lack of genuine connection with others.
- **Emotional burnout**: Constantly compromising your values or pretending to be someone you're not can be emotionally exhausting. You may find yourself feeling drained, overwhelmed, or disconnected from your own sense of purpose. This emotional burnout is often a sign that you're living out of alignment with your integrity.

The good news is that living out of integrity is not a permanent state. The key is to recognize when you've strayed from your values and to take action to bring yourself back into alignment.

Restoring Integrity: The Path to Realignment

Living with integrity is a practice—it requires regular reflection and a willingness to course-correct when you find yourself out of alignment.

No one is perfect, and there will inevitably be moments when you act in ways that don't reflect your values.

The important thing is not to avoid mistakes altogether but to recognize when you've strayed from your integrity and take steps to realign.

Here's how to restore integrity and realign with your values:

- **Acknowledge where you've strayed**: The first step to restoring integrity is recognizing where you've fallen out of alignment. This might be in a particular relationship, a work situation, or even in how you're treating yourself. Be honest with yourself about where you've compromised your values or acted in ways that don't reflect your true self.
- **Recommit to your values**: Take time to reconnect with your core values. These are the guiding principles that define who you are and how you want to live. By recommitting to your values, you're creating a clear path forward, grounded in what's most important to you.
- **Take responsibility for your actions**: If your actions have impacted others, it's important to take responsibility. This might involve apologizing, clarifying your intentions, or making amends in relationships where you've been out of integrity. Taking responsibility builds trust and helps restore authenticity in your interactions.
- **Create a plan to realign**: For each area where you've identified that you're out of alignment, create a specific plan to bring yourself back into integrity. This could involve changing your behavior, setting new boundaries, or making different decisions moving forward. The goal is to ensure that your future actions reflect your values.
- **Practice self-compassion**: It's easy to be hard on

yourself when you realize you've fallen out of integrity, but it's important to approach this process with compassion. Integrity is not about being perfect—it's about being honest with yourself and others, and making continuous efforts to live authentically.

Exercise: Identifying and Realigning Areas of Your Life

Today's exercise is designed to help you reflect on areas where you may have fallen out of integrity and create a plan to realign with your values.

This process will help you restore self-trust, strengthen your authenticity, and bring a deeper sense of coherence to your life.

Step 1: Identify Areas Where You're Out of Integrity

Begin by reflecting on different aspects of your life—your relationships, work, personal commitments, and self-care practices. Are there any areas where you feel you've compromised your values or acted out of alignment with your true self?

Here are some questions to guide your reflection:

- **Where have I acted in ways that don't reflect my core values?**
- **Are there relationships where I'm not showing up authentically?**
- **Have I made commitments that I haven't followed through on?**
- Do I feel internal conflict in any area of my life?

Step 2: Recommit to Your Values

Once you've identified areas where you've fallen out of alignment, take a moment to reconnect with your values. Write down the core values that matter most to you—whether it's honesty, compassion, integrity, or self-care.

Reaffirming your values helps ground you in your truth and provides a clear path for moving forward.

Step 3: Create a Plan to Realign

For each area where you've identified that you're out of integrity, create a specific plan to bring yourself back into alignment. This could involve having a difficult conversation, setting new boundaries, or changing your behavior in a particular situation.

The goal is to ensure that your future actions reflect your values.

Example:

- *"I've been avoiding conflict in my relationship by not expressing how I truly feel. My value is honesty, so I will have a conversation to address my concerns with kindness and respect."*
- *"I've been neglecting my personal health and well-being due to work stress. My value is self-care, so I will set aside time each day for exercise and reflection."*

Step 4: Reflect on How It Feels to Realign

Once you've completed the exercise, take a moment to reflect on how it feels to bring yourself back into integrity. Do you notice a sense of relief, peace, or clarity?

Realigning with your values strengthens your self-trust and helps you live with greater authenticity and confidence.

Reflection on the Exercise

How did it feel to reflect on areas where you may be out of integrity? Were there moments of clarity or realization?

By acknowledging where you've fallen out of alignment and taking steps to realign, you're actively building trust in yourself and creating a life that feels more coherent and meaningful.

Takeaway

Today, you've taken an important step in aligning your actions with your values and living in integrity with your true self. Living with integrity is not about perfection—it's about making choices that reflect who you are and what you believe.

By committing to this practice, you build self-trust, deepen your authenticity, and create a life that feels more aligned with your purpose.

As you move forward, remember that integrity is a journey, not a destination. It requires ongoing reflection and a willingness to make adjustments when needed.

But with each step, you grow closer to living a life that is truly in harmony with your values.

Tomorrow, we'll explore how to integrate everything you've learned throughout this journey so that you can continue living with authenticity, purpose, and integrity.

But for today, take a moment to appreciate the clarity and confidence that come from living in alignment with your true self.

Remember: *Living in integrity means acting in ways that reflect your values and true self. It builds trust, fosters inner peace, and helps you live a life that feels aligned and authentic.*

DAY 20: FINDING PEACE IN STILLNESS

Welcome to Day 20. As you approach the conclusion of this transformative journey, today's focus is on one of the most powerful yet overlooked tools for self-connection: *stillness*. In a world that moves so fast, filled with constant demands for our attention, learning how to be still can feel like a radical act of self-love.

In truth, stillness is where some of the deepest growth, healing, and self-connection occur.

Stillness is not about stopping all activity or emptying your mind of thoughts. It's about creating space—a quiet, inner sanctuary where you can reconnect with yourself, away from the noise, the distractions, and the endless to-do lists.

This stillness gives you the opportunity to listen to your inner voice, to breathe, and to be present with yourself, just as you are.

It is a way of touching the calm, peaceful core that exists within you, no matter what's happening in the world around you.

You've spent the past weeks embracing your authentic self, cultivating emotional resilience, and aligning your actions with your values.

Now, as you near the end of this 21-day journey, it's time to integrate everything by learning how to *be*—how to find peace, clarity, and strength in moments of stillness.

Today, we'll explore the importance of stillness for self-connection, how it can help you find peace in a chaotic world, and how to bring the practice of stillness into your daily life.

The Power of Stillness

In a society that values busyness and productivity, stillness can feel counterproductive. We're taught that we should always be doing something, improving ourselves, or achieving more. This constant push to do more can leave us disconnected from ourselves, overwhelmed by stress, and chasing external validation rather than cultivating internal peace.

Stillness offers a way to reclaim your energy, focus, and sense of self. It's a practice that allows you to step away from the demands of life and connect with the quiet, calm space within you.

This inner stillness is not just about relaxation; it's about reconnecting with the present moment, observing your thoughts and emotions without judgment, and discovering the clarity and wisdom that come from simply *being*.

Here's why stillness is so powerful:

- **It fosters deep self-awareness**: Stillness creates the space for reflection. When you slow down and stop doing, you become more attuned to your thoughts, emotions, and inner experiences. This heightened self-awareness is essential for personal growth and self-connection.
- **It builds emotional resilience**: Practicing stillness helps you develop a calm center that you can return to when life becomes overwhelming. It teaches you how to observe your emotions without being swept away by them, allowing you to respond to challenges with clarity and composure.
- **It enhances clarity and perspective**: Often, we get so caught up in the noise and busyness of life that we lose sight of what's truly important. Stillness allows you to gain

perspective on your life, your goals, and your relationships. It's in these quiet moments that solutions to problems often become clear, and you can refocus on what matters most.

- **It cultivates inner peace**: True peace comes from within, not from external circumstances. Stillness helps you access this peace by quieting the mind and grounding you in the present moment. Even in the midst of chaos, you can find a sense of calm and balance through stillness.

Stillness is not about escaping life; it's about connecting more deeply to it. It's about creating the space to listen to yourself, to breathe, and to rediscover the strength and clarity that reside within you.

Inner Peace and Authenticity: The Role of Stillness

When we talk about living authentically, we often focus on how we express our true selves through actions, decisions, and interactions with others. Authenticity also requires an inward journey—a process of becoming deeply connected to who you are in each moment. This deeper authenticity is found through stillness.

Stillness is a gateway to inner peace, and inner peace is essential for living authentically. When you cultivate inner peace, you create a foundation of calm and clarity that allows you to navigate life with greater ease, self-awareness, and authenticity. You're no longer reacting impulsively to external pressures or distractions. Instead, you're responding to life from a place of inner strength and groundedness.

Here's why inner peace is key to authenticity:

- **It connects you to your intuition**: In stillness, you can hear the quiet voice of your intuition—the part of you that knows what's right for you, even when external circumstances or opinions pull you in different directions. This connection to your inner wisdom helps guide your decisions and actions, allowing you to live in alignment with your true self.

- **It allows you to embrace the present moment**: Authenticity isn't just about expressing your true self; it's also about *being* fully present. When you're caught up in worries about the future or regrets about the past, it's easy to lose touch with who you are right now. Stillness helps ground you in the present, where you can fully embrace your authenticity.
- **It deepens self-compassion**: In stillness, you learn to sit with yourself without judgment. You become more compassionate toward your thoughts, emotions, and experiences, recognizing that they are all part of your journey. This self-compassion is a key component of authenticity because it allows you to accept yourself as you are, without striving for perfection.
- **It creates space for intentionality**: When you practice stillness, you create space to reflect on your life, your choices, and your behaviors. This reflection allows you to act more intentionally, rather than reacting impulsively or being driven by external forces. In this way, stillness helps you align your actions with your values and live more authentically.

Stillness is a practice of returning to yourself. It allows you to step away from the noise and distractions of life and reconnect with your inner truth.

In this space, you can listen to your intuition, embrace your present reality, and find peace in simply *being* who you are.

The Challenge of Embracing Stillness in a Busy World

In today's fast-paced world, finding stillness can feel like a challenge. We're constantly bombarded with information, distractions, and the pressure to be productive.

Even when we do have moments of quiet, our minds may still be racing, filled with thoughts about what we should be doing or what comes next.

Learning to embrace stillness in the midst of a busy life is one of the most transformative things you can do for yourself.

Stillness isn't about creating a perfect environment free of distractions; it's about cultivating an inner calm that you can access anywhere, anytime. It's about learning to be present with yourself, even when the world around you feels chaotic.

Here are some common challenges you may face when practicing stillness, and how to overcome them:

- **Restlessness**: When you first begin practicing stillness, you may feel restless or impatient. Your mind might wander, or you might feel the urge to move on to the next task. This is completely normal. Instead of fighting the restlessness, acknowledge it and gently bring your focus back to the present moment. Over time, you'll find it easier to sit with yourself in stillness.
- **Overthinking**: Stillness can sometimes bring up thoughts or emotions that you've been avoiding. You may find yourself ruminating on the past or worrying about the future. When this happens, remember that the goal of stillness is not to eliminate your thoughts but to observe them without attachment. Let your thoughts come and go like passing clouds, and bring your attention back to your breath or the present moment.
- **The pressure to be productive**: In a culture that values productivity, it can be hard to justify taking time for stillness. You may feel like you're wasting time by not doing something "useful." But stillness is far from idle. It's a powerful practice that helps you recharge, gain clarity, and

strengthen your connection to yourself. Trust that stillness is a valuable part of your personal growth and well-being, even if it doesn't result in immediate, tangible outcomes.

Stillness is not about perfection. It's about showing up for yourself, even when it's uncomfortable or challenging. The more you practice, the more you'll discover the profound peace and strength that stillness brings.

Exercise: Cultivating Stillness through Meditation or Breathwork

Today's exercise is an invitation to experience the power of stillness firsthand. Through a simple meditation or breathwork practice, you'll cultivate inner stillness, reconnect with your breath, and discover the peace that comes from being present with yourself.

Step 1: Create a Calming Environment

Find a quiet space where you can sit comfortably for 10 minutes without interruptions. You may want to dim the lights, light a candle, or play soft, calming music to help create a peaceful atmosphere. Choose a seated position that allows your spine to be straight but relaxed—this could be sitting cross-legged on the floor or sitting upright in a chair with your feet flat on the ground.

Step 2: Set an Intention

Before you begin, take a moment to set a simple intention for this practice. Your intention could be to cultivate inner stillness, to reconnect with your breath, or simply to be present with yourself. This intention will help guide your focus and bring deeper meaning to the practice.

Step 3: Focus on Your Breath

Close your eyes and bring your attention to your breath. Begin by taking a few deep breaths, inhaling slowly through your nose and exhaling through your mouth.

As you continue to breathe, let your breath settle into a natural rhythm.

Focus on the sensation of the air entering and leaving your body—the rise and fall of your chest or the gentle expansion and contraction of your abdomen.

Step 4: Observe Your Thoughts

As you sit in stillness, you may notice thoughts or emotions arising. This is completely natural.

The goal is not to clear your mind of all thoughts, but to observe them without attachment. Imagine each thought as a cloud passing through the sky of your mind. Acknowledge it, and then gently return your focus to your breath.

If you find your mind wandering, don't judge yourself. Simply bring your awareness back to the present moment, using your breath as an anchor.

Step 5: Embrace the Stillness

As you continue to focus on your breath, allow yourself to sink deeper into the stillness.

Notice the spaces between your thoughts, the moments of quiet where you are fully present. In this space, there's nothing to do, nowhere to go—just you, your breath, and the stillness within. Allow yourself to rest in this state of peace and presence.

Step 6: Reflect on the Experience

After 10 minutes, gently bring your awareness back to the room. Take a few deep breaths, and when you're ready, open your eyes.

Take a moment to reflect on how you feel after the practice. Do you notice a sense of calm, clarity, or inner peace? What did you observe about yourself during the stillness?

Reflection on the Exercise

How did it feel to practice stillness? Did you notice moments of restlessness, clarity, or peace? Stillness is a practice, and like any practice, it takes time to develop.

Each time you engage with stillness, you strengthen your ability to connect with yourself, to find peace in the present moment, and to navigate life with greater clarity and resilience.

Takeaway

Today, you've experienced the power of stillness—a practice that allows you to reconnect with your inner peace, no matter what's happening in your external world.

Stillness is a simple yet profound tool for self-connection. It creates space for you to pause, reflect, and rediscover the calm and clarity that already exist within you.

As you move forward on this journey, remember that stillness is always available to you. In moments of stress, overwhelm, or uncertainty, you can return to this practice of stillness.

Whether through meditation, breathwork, or simply taking a moment to sit quietly with yourself, stillness will help you ground yourself, regain clarity, and reconnect with your true self.

Tomorrow, we'll conclude this 21-day journey by integrating everything you've learned and celebrating the transformation you've experienced.

For today just take a moment to honor the peace and presence you've cultivated within yourself.

Remember: *Stillness is where you find the clarity, peace, and strength to live authentically. In the quiet moments, you reconnect with the calm and wisdom that already exist within you.*

DAY 21: CELEBRATING YOUR JOURNEY

Welcome to Day 21. You've reached a significant milestone, a moment of deep reflection and celebration.

Over the past three weeks, you've taken bold steps toward reconnecting with your true self, building resilience, cultivating self-compassion, and aligning your life with your values.

Today is a day to pause, honor your growth, and celebrate everything you've accomplished.

This journey hasn't been just about making surface-level changes—it's been a transformational experience of personal growth, self-discovery, and learning to embrace your authenticity.

Through these daily practices, you've peeled back layers, confronted challenges, and connected with the core of who you are. You've engaged in meaningful exercises, deep reflections, and moments of stillness, all designed to help you build a life grounded in integrity, purpose, and emotional resilience.

Today, we're not simply marking the end of a 21-day program. This is a time to celebrate the beginning of a lifelong commitment to your personal growth and well-being. This journey doesn't end here.

You've cultivated the tools, awareness, and practices that will continue to support you as you grow, evolve, and thrive in your authentic life.

Let's take time to reflect on where you started, where you are now, and where you're heading.

This final day is about acknowledging the transformation you've undergone, celebrating your achievements, and setting clear, purposeful intentions for the future.

Reflecting on Your Journey

Over the past three weeks, you've explored what it means to be truly connected to yourself. You've embarked on an inward journey, taking the time to listen to your thoughts, honor your emotions, and understand the layers of your identity. You've practiced self-acceptance, learning to love not just the polished parts of yourself, but also the imperfections and vulnerabilities that make you beautifully human.

Here's a look at some of the key areas where you've grown:

- **Self-Connection**: You began this journey by meeting your true self, distinguishing between the roles you play and the authentic self that lies beneath them. You've worked to peel away the layers of societal expectations and external pressures, discovering the unique person you are at your core. By reconnecting with your values, you've aligned yourself with what matters most, creating a foundation for living a life that reflects your true essence.
- **Emotional Resilience**: Throughout the program, you've built emotional resilience by learning to sit with discomfort, manage emotional triggers, and develop self-compassion. You've set healthy boundaries, released emotional baggage, and built self-trust, allowing you to approach life's challenges with greater strength and flexibility. You've also learned how to cultivate self-kindness, offering yourself the grace to grow, stumble, and evolve without harsh self-judgment.
- **Living Authentically**: You've explored what it means

to live in alignment with your values and true self. From embracing your imperfections to practicing vulnerability, you've taken steps to embody authenticity in your daily life. You've made choices that reflect who you are, rather than who you feel you "should" be. By living with integrity, you've built trust in yourself and created more meaningful connections with others.

- **Inner Peace**: One of the most profound discoveries on this journey has been the power of stillness. You've learned how to cultivate moments of peace and presence, even in the midst of life's chaos. Through mindfulness, breathwork, and self-reflection, you've connected with the deep inner peace that resides within you, regardless of external circumstances. This practice of stillness has become a wellspring of clarity, strength, and grounding for you.

As you reflect on the journey, it's important to acknowledge the courage it took to engage with these practices. Growth is never easy, and personal transformation requires vulnerability, patience, and persistence. However, you've shown up for yourself in ways that will continue to bear fruit long after this program ends.

The Transformation You've Experienced

Let's take a closer look at the transformation you've undergone. Personal growth isn't always visible on the surface—it often happens quietly, within.

However, the subtle shifts in your mindset, emotional patterns, and behaviors have a profound impact on your overall well-being and how you move through the world.

Here's a breakdown of some of the key changes you may have noticed:

- **Greater Self-Awareness**: You've developed a deeper understanding of your inner world—your thoughts, emotions, triggers, and patterns. This heightened self-awareness has allowed you to make more intentional choices, responding to situations with clarity rather than reacting impulsively. You've also become more attuned to your needs, desires, and boundaries, empowering you to take better care of yourself.
- **Improved Emotional Regulation**: By practicing mindfulness, emotional reflection, and resilience, you've gained tools to better manage difficult emotions. Rather than being overwhelmed by stress, anger, or anxiety, you now have the capacity to observe these emotions with compassion, allowing them to flow through you without taking control. This emotional regulation has strengthened your ability to navigate challenges with calm and grace.
- **Increased Confidence and Self-Trust**: Living in alignment with your values has reinforced your confidence and self-trust. You know that you can rely on yourself to make decisions that honor your truth, even in the face of external pressures. This inner confidence is not based on external validation but rooted in your authentic self, providing a sense of empowerment that comes from within.
- **Enhanced Relationships**: As you've become more connected to yourself, you've likely noticed a shift in your relationships. By showing up authentically, setting boundaries, and communicating openly, you've deepened your connections with those around you. Authentic relationships thrive on vulnerability and honesty, and your willingness to express your true self has created more meaningful, fulfilling interactions with others.
- **Inner Peace and Balance**: Perhaps one of the most rewarding aspects of this journey has been the cultivation of inner peace. Through stillness, meditation,

and breathwork, you've discovered a well of calm and serenity that you can access at any time. This inner peace has brought balance to your life, helping you stay grounded in the present moment and centered in your true self.

This transformation is something to be proud of. It's the result of your commitment to your personal growth, your willingness to engage in deep self-reflection, and your dedication to creating a life that reflects your most authentic self.

Setting Intentions for Continued Growth

As you celebrate your progress, it's also important to look ahead and set intentions for the future.

Personal growth is an ongoing journey, and the insights and practices you've gained over the past 21 days will continue to support you as you evolve.

Setting clear intentions helps you stay grounded in your growth and ensures that the momentum you've built continues to propel you forward.

Here are some questions to guide your intention-setting:

- **What practices have been most meaningful to you, and how will you continue to prioritize them?**
  Reflect on the tools, exercises, or reflections that resonated most with you. These practices are the ones that will continue to support your growth. Whether it's daily meditation, journaling, or setting boundaries, identify the habits you want to carry forward and integrate into your everyday life.
- **How will you continue to live in alignment with your authentic self?**
  Living authentically is a lifelong practice. Think about how you can continue to honor your values and express your

true self in all areas of your life—whether in relationships, at work, or in personal pursuits. What specific actions will you take to ensure that you remain true to yourself?

- **What challenges might you face, and how can you navigate them with the tools you've learned?**
Growth is not linear, and there will be moments when you're tested. Reflect on potential challenges—whether internal (self-doubt, fear, or old patterns) or external (pressure from others, life's uncertainties). How can you use the tools you've gained—such as self-compassion, emotional resilience, or mindfulness—to stay grounded during these challenges?
- **What are your hopes and dreams for the future?**
Consider what you want to manifest in the coming months or years. These could be personal goals, career aspirations, or ways you want to deepen your relationships. Think about how you want to continue growing, what kind of life you want to build, and how you can keep nurturing your inner peace and authenticity.

By setting these intentions, you're not only honoring the work you've done but also creating a clear path for continued growth.

These intentions will serve as guiding lights, reminding you of the progress you've made and the direction you're heading.

Exercise: Reflecting on Your Journey and Setting Future Intentions

Today's exercise invites you to reflect on the entire 21-day journey and celebrate your growth. It's also an opportunity to set powerful intentions for your continued personal development.

Step 1: Reflect on Your Growth

Take a few moments to look back on the past three weeks. Write a reflection on how you've grown, the challenges you've overcome, and the insights you've gained. Celebrate the moments of transformation, no matter how big or small.

Here are some prompts to guide your reflection:

- **What have I learned about myself on this journey?**
- **What practices have been the most impactful for me?**
- **In what ways have I changed emotionally, mentally, or spiritually?**
- **How do I feel more connected to myself and my values?**

Step 2: Celebrate Your Progress

As you reflect on your journey, take time to celebrate your accomplishments. Write a letter to yourself, acknowledging the progress you've made, the effort you've invested, and the transformation you've experienced.

This is a moment to honor the growth you've worked so hard for and to remind yourself of the strength and resilience you've cultivated.

Step 3: Set Intentions for Future Growth

Now, look ahead. What are your intentions for the next phase of your journey? Write down clear, specific intentions that will guide your continued personal development. Think about the practices you want to carry forward, the goals you want to achieve, and the ways you want to stay connected to your authentic self.

Use these prompts to guide your intention-setting:

- **What practices will I continue to prioritize in my daily life?**
- **How will I stay connected to my true self moving forward?**
- **What are my goals for personal growth over the next few months?**
- **How can I continue to cultivate self-compassion,**

resilience, and inner peace?

Reflection on the Exercise

How did it feel to reflect on your journey and celebrate your growth? What insights did you gain from setting intentions for the future?

This final reflection and intention-setting process solidifies the work you've done, ensuring that the transformation you've experienced continues to unfold in meaningful ways.

Takeaway

Today marks the end of this 21-day journey, but it is truly the beginning of a lifelong commitment to your personal growth, well-being, and authenticity.

You've spent the past three weeks reconnecting with yourself, building resilience, and learning to live in alignment with your values. This is something to celebrate.

The tools you've gained—self-compassion, emotional resilience, mindfulness, and stillness—will continue to support you as you navigate the complexities of life.

Personal growth is not a linear path, but you now have the foundation to face challenges with strength, navigate change with grace, and continue evolving as the person you are meant to be.

As you move forward, remember that this journey is ongoing. There will be moments of challenge, but there will also be moments of incredible growth, joy, and self-discovery.

You are more than capable of continuing this journey, and the progress you've made will carry you forward into a life that reflects your most authentic self.

Celebrate your journey. Celebrate your strength, resilience, and commitment to yourself.

And as you move into this next chapter, know that you have everything you need to live a life of authenticity, peace, and purpose.

Remember: *This is not the end—it's the beginning. Continue to honor your journey, celebrate your growth, and embrace the unfolding path ahead. You are more than capable of living a life of authenticity, inner peace, and purpose.*

CONCLUSION: YOUR NEXT STEPS

As you stand at the end of this 21-day journey, it's important to recognize that the work you've done over these past three weeks is not the end—it's a beginning. You've cultivated new practices, developed deeper self-awareness, and strengthened your connection to your authentic self, but this is just the start of an ongoing process of growth.

Self-connection is not something that can be checked off a list or completed in a set amount of time. It is a lifelong practice—one that will evolve with you as you continue to learn, grow, and experience life's changes.

Each of the tools, exercises, and reflections you've explored are designed to support you not just now, but for the long haul. Personal growth isn't linear; it ebbs and flows.

There will be times when you feel deeply connected to yourself and others, and times when you may feel lost or disconnected. The key is to approach this journey with compassion and patience, knowing that self-connection is a practice you return to, again and again, throughout your life.

In this final chapter, we'll explore how to maintain the momentum you've gained, track your personal progress, and stay aligned with your core values. You'll also learn how to engage with a community that can support your continued growth.

Remember, this journey isn't something you have to go through alone—there is great power in sharing your experiences with others who are also committed to their personal development.

Let's dive into the next steps on your journey of self-connection, growth, and authenticity.

Continuing the Journey: Self-Connection as an Ongoing Practice

One of the most important lessons of this journey is that self-connection is an ongoing practice. The progress you've made is significant, but the insights and changes you've experienced are just the beginning. The practices you've learned—whether it's stillness, mindfulness, emotional reflection, or boundary setting—are lifelong tools. These are practices you can revisit and deepen over time.

As you continue, it's important to keep in mind that this work doesn't require perfection. There will be moments when you feel completely in tune with yourself and your emotions, and others when you feel disconnected or off-course. That's okay.

The goal is not to achieve an ideal state of self-connection but to cultivate a consistent practice of checking in with yourself, honoring your needs, and taking small steps toward growth.

Here are a few ways to continue your journey of self-connection:

- **Return to the exercises**: The exercises and reflections you've done over the past three weeks aren't one-time activities. They are tools you can return to whenever you feel the need to reconnect with yourself. Whether you're journaling about your core values, practicing stillness, or writing a compassionate letter to yourself, these exercises are designed to be revisited as your life changes and evolves. Each time you engage with them, you'll likely

discover new layers of insight and awareness.
- **Incorporate reflection into your routine**: Personal growth happens most powerfully when we make space for regular reflection. Carve out time in your schedule—whether it's weekly, monthly, or quarterly—to sit with yourself and reflect on how you're feeling, where you've grown, and what areas might need more attention. This can be as simple as journaling for 10 minutes or spending a few moments in quiet reflection at the end of each day. By making reflection a regular practice, you'll stay grounded in your self-connection and ensure that you're continuing to align with your values.
- **Embrace the ebb and flow**: Growth isn't always a straight line. There will be times when you feel deeply connected to yourself, and other times when life's demands, challenges, or distractions may pull you away. That's natural. The key is to remain compassionate with yourself, embracing the natural ebb and flow of personal growth. When you notice yourself feeling disconnected, use the tools you've learned to gently bring yourself back to center. Self-connection is a practice of returning—returning to your breath, to your values, to your inner wisdom.

Tracking Your Progress: Maintaining Momentum

One of the most powerful ways to ensure continued growth is by regularly tracking your progress. This doesn't need to be a rigid or formal process, but simply a way to acknowledge how far you've come, identify patterns, and celebrate your wins.

Personal growth is often a gradual process, and without tracking it, it can be easy to overlook the small yet significant changes that occur over time.

Here are some ways to track your personal growth:

- **Personal Growth Journal**: Dedicate a journal specifically to your self-connection journey. Use this journal to document your reflections, challenges, insights, and growth. You can write about specific exercises you've revisited, record your thoughts after a meditation session, or reflect on how you handled a challenging situation.

  At the end of each month, review your journal entries to notice patterns, progress, or areas where you'd like to focus more attention.
  Consider using prompts to guide your journaling:
    - What have I learned about myself this month?
    - How have I aligned my actions with my core values?
    - What challenges have I faced, and what strengths have I discovered through them?
- **Revisit Your Values**: Your core values are the compass guiding your life. Make it a regular practice to revisit them—perhaps once every three months. Reflect on whether your values are still the same, whether they've evolved, or whether new values have emerged. Check in with how you're living in alignment with these values. If you notice any areas where you've drifted, use this reflection as an opportunity to realign your actions with what matters most.
- **Set Monthly Intentions**: At the start of each month, set clear, achievable intentions for your personal growth. These could be simple, actionable steps, such as practicing daily mindfulness or setting a new boundary in a relationship. At the end of the month, reflect on how you've honored these intentions and what adjustments you'd like to make for the following month. This process of setting and reflecting on intentions helps keep you focused and intentional in your growth.
- **Celebrate Milestones**: Growth happens in small steps, and it's important to celebrate each milestone along the

way. When you successfully establish a new boundary, practice self-compassion in a challenging moment, or simply make time for stillness, take a moment to celebrate. These victories—no matter how small they may seem—are meaningful markers of progress. Celebrating them helps you stay motivated and reinforces the positive changes you've made.

The Community Connection: Strength in Sharing the Journey

While self-connection is a deeply personal process, it's also one that can be greatly enhanced by community. Sharing your journey with others who are also committed to their personal growth creates a supportive environment where you can exchange insights, offer encouragement, and celebrate progress together.

Building connections with like-minded individuals helps sustain your motivation and provides a sense of belonging, reminding you that you're not alone on this path.

Here are a few ways to find or create a community that supports your growth:

- **Join Online Communities**: The internet is full of online communities dedicated to personal growth, mindfulness, and self-development. These forums or social media groups provide a space where you can connect with others who are on a similar journey. Whether it's a Facebook group, a personal growth forum, or a wellness community on Instagram, joining an online space can help you exchange ideas, ask questions, and learn from others' experiences. Engaging with a virtual community can be particularly helpful if you live in an area where local resources are limited.

- **Attend Workshops or Events**: Many cities offer in-person events focused on personal growth, mindfulness, and wellness. These workshops or retreats can provide an immersive experience where you can connect with others who share your interests and values. Whether it's a mindfulness meditation retreat, a self-care workshop, or an emotional resilience class, these events offer an opportunity to deepen your practice and build real-life connections with others.

- **Start a Discussion Group**: If you can't find a community that resonates with you, consider creating one of your own. Starting a discussion group—whether in-person or virtual—can provide a space for meaningful conversations about growth, self-connection, and well-being. You might meet monthly to share reflections, discuss books or podcasts, and support each other in your personal growth journeys. Creating a group like this not only fosters connection but also reinforces your own commitment to growth.
- **Find an Accountability Partner**: If you prefer more intimate support, consider finding one person to be your accountability partner. This could be a friend, family member, or someone you've met through an online community. Check in with each other regularly—whether weekly or monthly—to share your reflections, offer encouragement, and hold each other accountable for your personal growth goals. Having someone to share your journey with can be incredibly motivating, providing both support and accountability as you continue to evolve.

Final Thoughts: Your Journey Continues

As you step forward from this 21-day journey, remember that the work you've done here is not about arriving at a final destination. Personal growth and self-connection are ongoing practices—ones that you can continue to nurture and deepen for the rest of your life.

This journey is about being present with yourself, honoring your needs, and taking small, intentional steps toward living a life that reflects your true values and desires.

There will be moments of clarity and moments of uncertainty, times of deep connection and times when you feel disconnected.

The important thing is to return to yourself, again and again, with compassion, patience, and curiosity. Trust that the practices you've developed here will continue to support you, even in the most challenging moments.

As you move forward, stay open to the process. Growth is rarely linear, and it's okay if you don't have all the answers right away. What matters is that you're committed to the journey—that you're willing to show up for yourself, to listen, and to grow.

You've already done something remarkable by taking this time to focus on your personal growth. Celebrate that commitment. Celebrate the courage it took to dive deep, to reflect, and to embrace your authentic self. You've laid a strong foundation, and from here, the possibilities for continued growth are limitless.

Your Next Steps: A Recap

1. **Continue the Practice**: Self-connection is a lifelong process. Revisit the exercises, reflect regularly, and stay open to growth.
2. **Track Your Progress**: Use tools like journaling, revisiting your values, and setting monthly intentions to track your personal growth. Celebrate your milestones, no matter how small they seem.
3. **Find Community**: Share your journey with others by joining an online group, attending workshops, or finding an accountability partner. Connection strengthens your growth.

Takeaway: The Journey Is Yours

As you close the final chapter of this 21-day program, take a moment to acknowledge yourself. You've done something truly powerful. You've shown up for yourself, explored your inner world, and committed to a journey of self-connection and growth. This is no small feat.

Remember, you don't have to do this perfectly, and you don't have to do it all at once. The journey of self-connection is yours to shape, moment by moment, day by day. You have everything you need within you to live a life that reflects your authentic self—one filled with purpose, resilience, and inner peace.

This is not the end—it's the beginning. Continue to honor your journey, celebrate your growth, and embrace the unfolding path ahead. You are capable of living a life of authenticity, inner peace, and purpose. And that journey begins anew every day.

Remember: *You are enough.*

BONUS SECTION: QUICK TOOLS FOR DAILY SELF-CONNECTION

As you continue on your journey of self-connection, it's important to have simple, effective tools that you can use in your daily life—especially when time is limited.

These quick tools are designed to help you stay connected to yourself, even amidst a busy schedule. Whether you need a moment of mindfulness, an empowering affirmation, or a way to track your emotional triggers, these resources will support you in maintaining your personal growth and emotional well-being.

In this bonus section, you'll find four practical tools to integrate into your daily routine:

- **Daily Affirmations**: Short, empowering affirmations to support self-compassion and resilience.
- **Mindfulness Prompts**: Simple prompts to guide you toward mindfulness and self-reflection each day.
- **Emotional Trigger Tracker**: A tool for identifying, managing, and overcoming emotional triggers.
- **Self-Care Checklist**: A guide for integrating self-care into your life, even with a busy schedule.

Each of these tools is designed to be flexible and easy to incorporate into your day, providing quick and powerful ways to stay connected with yourself.

Daily Affirmations: Empowering Self-Compassion and Resilience

Affirmations are simple yet powerful statements that help rewire your mindset, boost self-compassion, and build resilience.

By repeating affirmations, you're training your mind to focus on positive, empowering thoughts rather than self-doubt or criticism. These affirmations are designed to support your emotional well-being and strengthen your connection to your authentic self.

You can use these affirmations as part of your morning routine, during moments of stress, or whenever you need a reminder of your inner strength.

Sample Daily Affirmations:

- *"I am enough, just as I am."*
  This affirmation helps you embrace self-acceptance and compassion, reminding you that you are worthy simply because of who you are—not because of what you do or achieve.
- *"I trust myself to make the right decisions for my life."*
  This affirmation reinforces self-trust and reminds you that you have the wisdom within to guide your path.
- *"I am resilient, and I grow stronger with each challenge I face."*
  This affirmation empowers you to see challenges as opportunities for growth and reminds you of your inner strength.
- *"I choose to release what no longer serves me."*
  Whether it's a limiting belief, a toxic relationship, or a past

hurt, this affirmation encourages you to let go of anything that weighs you down.
- *"I am worthy of love, care, and attention."*
This affirmation nurtures self-love and reminds you to prioritize your own well-being, even when life gets busy.

Mindfulness Prompts: Simple Practices for Daily Reflection

Mindfulness is one of the most effective ways to stay present and connected to yourself throughout the day. By practicing mindfulness, you become more aware of your thoughts, feelings, and environment, allowing you to respond with intention rather than reacting automatically.

These prompts are designed to bring moments of reflection and awareness into your daily routine, helping you stay grounded and in tune with your emotions.

Here are simple mindfulness prompts you can use each day. You can reflect on these prompts in a journal or simply take a few moments to consider them throughout the day.

Sample Mindfulness Prompts:

- **Morning Mindfulness:**
  "What is one intention I want to set for today?"
  This prompt invites you to start your day with a clear intention, whether it's practicing patience, focusing on gratitude, or being present in your interactions.
- **Afternoon Check-In:**
  "What emotions am I feeling in this moment, and how can I hold space for them without judgment?"
  This midday check-in helps you become aware of your emotional state and encourages self-compassion by allowing your feelings to exist without trying to change or suppress them.
- **Evening Reflection:**

"What is one thing I learned about myself today?"
This prompt encourages you to reflect on the day's experiences and find moments of growth, no matter how small.

- **Body Scan**:
"How does my body feel right now? What areas need attention or care?"
A body scan is a simple way to reconnect with your physical self, noticing any areas of tension, stress, or discomfort, and offering those areas the care they need.

- **Gratitude Moment**:
"What is one thing I am grateful for right now?"
This prompt helps shift your focus to the positive, reminding you to appreciate the small joys in everyday life.

Emotional Trigger Tracker: A Tool for Understanding and Managing Triggers

Emotional triggers are situations, people, or events that evoke strong emotional reactions in us—often more intense than the situation warrants. Understanding your triggers is a key step in building emotional resilience and maintaining self-connection.

This Emotional Trigger Tracker is designed to help you identify and manage your triggers, so you can respond to challenging situations with more awareness and intention.

By tracking your emotional responses over time, you'll gain insight into what triggers you, how those triggers affect your behavior, and what strategies help you manage them effectively.

How to Use the Emotional Trigger Tracker:

1. **Identify the Trigger**:
Reflect on moments when you felt a strong emotional reaction—whether it was anger, frustration, anxiety,

or sadness. What was the situation, and what do you think triggered your response? Be as specific as possible.
2. **Record Your Response**:
Once you've identified the trigger, write down how you responded emotionally and physically. Did you feel your heart race, your body tense, or your mood change quickly? How did you behave in response to the trigger?
3. **Reflect on Underlying Beliefs**:
Emotional triggers often stem from underlying beliefs or past experiences. Ask yourself: *Why did this trigger such a strong reaction in me? What deeper belief or fear might be at play here?* This step helps you gain insight into the root causes of your emotional triggers.
4. **Develop Coping Strategies**:
Based on your reflection, consider how you might respond differently next time. What coping strategies—such as deep breathing, stepping away from the situation, or reframing your thoughts—can you use to manage the trigger more effectively?

Example Emotional Trigger Tracker:

Trigger	Emotional Response	Underlying Belief	Coping Strategy
A colleague criticizes my work in front of others.	Anger, embarrassment, feeling defensive	*"I'm not good enough"* or *"I need to prove myself to others."*	Take a deep breath, acknowledge the emotion, and respond calmly later.
Receiving a message from an ex-partner.	Anxiety, sadness	*"I'm afraid of being hurt again."*	Step away, practice self-compassion, and focus on the present.

Using the Emotional Trigger Tracker regularly will help you build emotional awareness and resilience over time. You'll learn to identify patterns, understand the underlying beliefs driving your reactions, and develop healthier ways to respond.

Self-Care Checklist: Integrating Self-Care into Busy Days

Self-care is an essential part of staying connected to yourself, but it's often the first thing to be neglected when life gets busy.

This Self-Care Checklist is designed to help you integrate small, meaningful self-care practices into your daily routine, even when your schedule feels overwhelming. By checking in with yourself regularly, you'll ensure that you're taking care of your mental, emotional, and physical well-being.

Daily Self-Care Checklist:

- **Physical Self-Care:**
  - *Move your body in a way that feels good.*
    Whether it's a walk, yoga, stretching, or dancing in your living room, make time to move your body daily. Physical movement helps release tension, boosts your mood, and strengthens your connection to your body.
  - *Hydrate throughout the day.*
    Drinking water is a simple but essential part of self-care. Keep a water bottle nearby and take regular sips to stay hydrated.
  - *Get enough rest.*
    Prioritize sleep and rest, even on busy days. Aim for 7-8 hours of sleep, and if that's not possible, take short breaks to recharge during the day.
- **Emotional Self-Care:**
  - *Check in with your emotions.*
    Throughout the day, pause and ask yourself how you're feeling emotionally. Acknowledge your feelings without judgment, and give yourself permission to feel what you're feeling.
  - *Practice self-compassion.*
    When you're facing a challenge or feeling down,

remind yourself that it's okay to make mistakes and that growth takes time. Speak to yourself kindly, as you would a close friend.
- **Mental Self-Care:**
    - *Take a break from screens.*
    Set aside time each day to step away from your phone, computer, or television. Give your mind a break from constant stimulation, and enjoy a moment of silence or reflection.
    - *Engage in a creative activity.*
    Whether it's writing, drawing, cooking, or playing music, engaging in creative activities helps stimulate your mind and provides an outlet for self-expression.
- **Spiritual Self-Care:**
    - *Spend time in nature.*
    Nature has a grounding and healing effect. Whether it's a short walk outside or simply sitting by a window, spending time in nature helps you reconnect with the world around you.
    - *Cultivate gratitude.*
    At the end of each day, write down or reflect on three things you're grateful for. Focusing on gratitude shifts your perspective toward the positive and helps you appreciate the small joys in life.

This checklist is a reminder that self-care doesn't have to be complicated or time-consuming. Small, consistent actions can make a big difference in your well-being. By incorporating these practices into your daily routine, you'll stay connected to yourself, even during life's busiest moments.

Final Thoughts

These Quick Tools for Daily Self-Connection are meant to be your go-to resources for maintaining self-compassion, mindfulness, emotional awareness, and self-care. Use them as needed, adapting them to fit your lifestyle and evolving needs.

Remember, self-connection is not about perfection—it's about taking small, intentional steps each day to nurture your relationship with yourself. The more you practice these tools, the deeper your connection to yourself will grow.

Carry these tools with you as you continue your journey, knowing that self-care, mindfulness, and emotional resilience are always within reach. You are worthy of love, attention, and care—each and every day.

www.ingramcontent.com/pod-product-compliance
Lightning Source LLC
Chambersburg PA
CBHW052155220526
45471CB00004B/1685